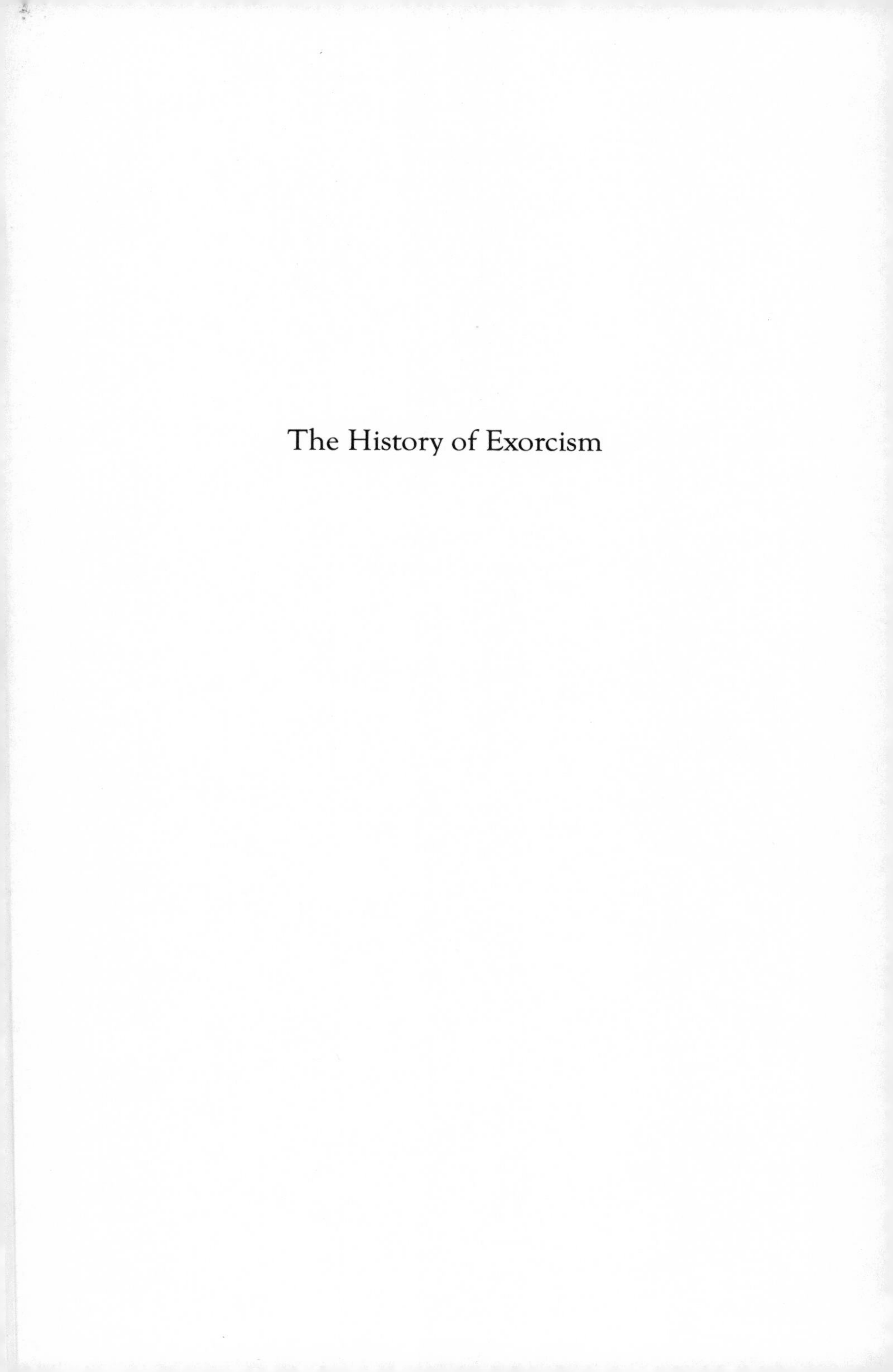

The History of Exorcism

Other books by Adam Blai
from Sophia Institute Press:

The Exorcism Files

The Catholic Guide to Miracles

Adam Blai

The History of Exorcism

SOPHIA INSTITUTE PRESS
Manchester, New Hampshire

Cover by Enrique J. Aguilar.

Cover images: *The Torment of Saint Anthony*, by Michelangelo,
courtesy of Wikimedia Commons; Baroque crucifix,
courtesy of Jorge Royan / Wikimedia Commons.

Sophia Institute Press
Box 5284, Manchester, NH 03108
1-800-888-9344
www.SophiaInstitute.com

Sophia Institute Press® is a registered trademark of Sophia Institute.

paperback ISBN 978-1-64413-932-5

ebook ISBN 978-1-64413-933-2

Library of Congress Control Number: 2023939933

First printing

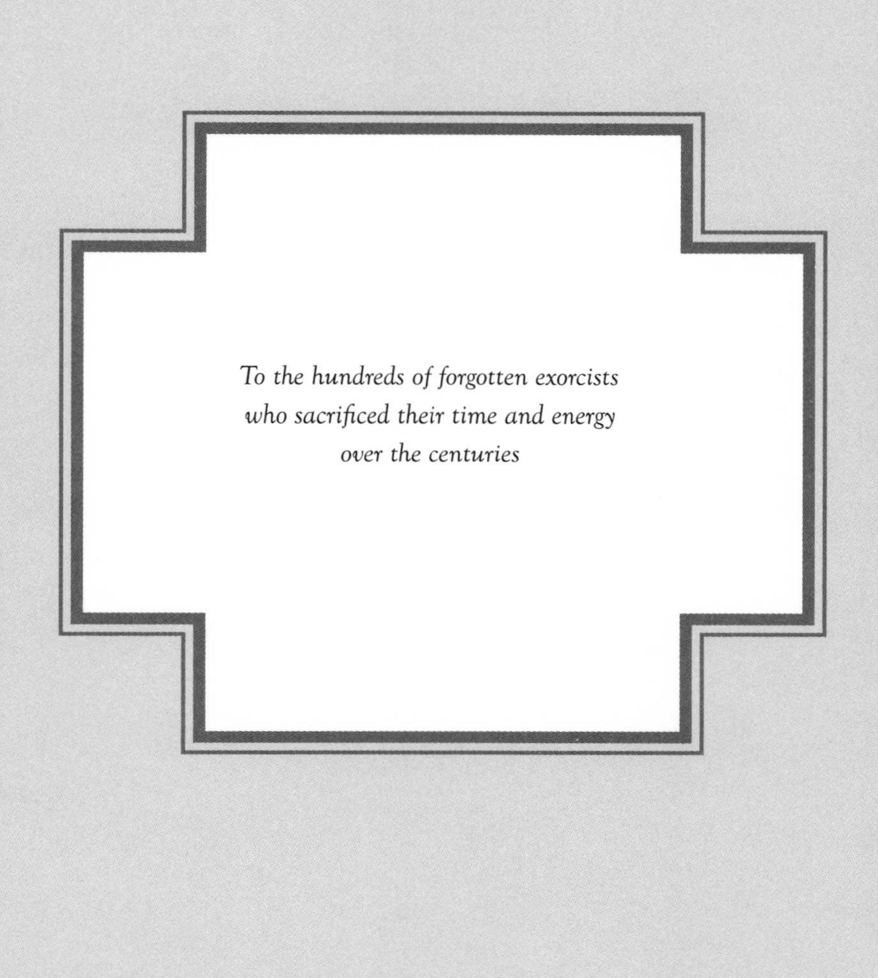

To the hundreds of forgotten exorcists
who sacrificed their time and energy
over the centuries

Contents

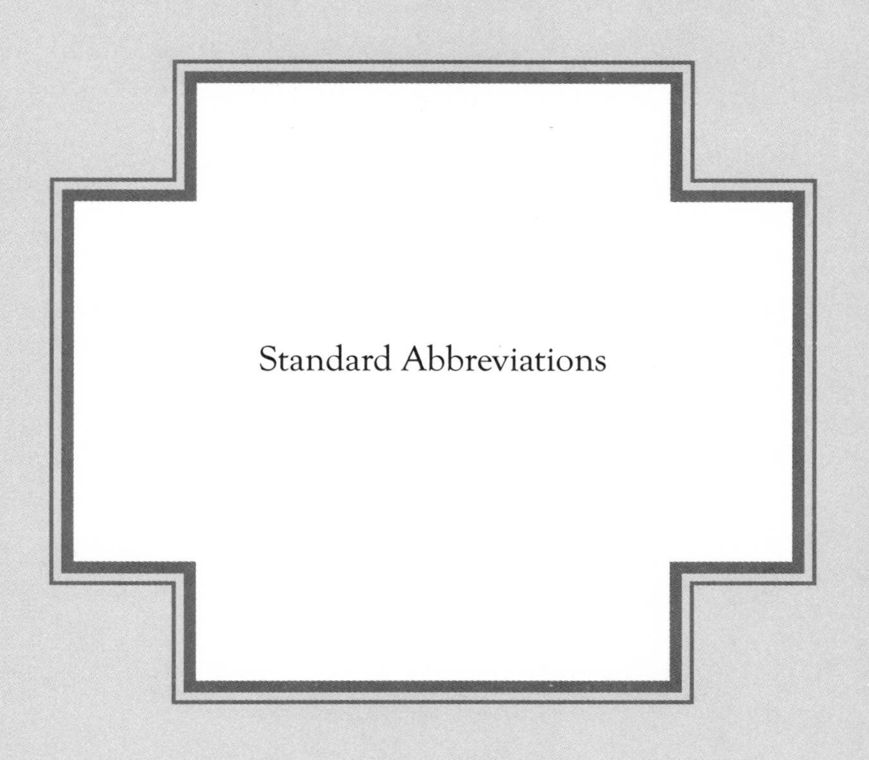

Standard Abbreviations

+

AAS	*Acta apostolicae sedis*
c.	canon
cc.	canons
CDWDS	Congregation for Divine Worship and Discipline of the Sacraments
CIC 17	*Codex iuris canonici, Pii X Pontificis Maximi iussu digestus*
CIC	*Codex iuris canonici, auctoritate Ioannis Pauli PP. II promulgates*
CLD	*Canon Law Digest*
CLSA	Canon Law Society of America
Flannery 1	A. Flannery, O.P., ed., *Vatican Council II*, vol. 1: *The Conciliar and Postconciliar Documents*, new rev. ed. (Northport, NY: Costello, 1998)
J	*The Jurist*
OR	*Les* Ordines Romani *du Haut Moyen Âge*, ed. M. Andrieu, 5 vols. (Louvain: Spicilegium Sacrum Lovaniense, 1931–1961)
PG	*Patrologia curcus completes, series Graeca*, ed. J.-P. Migne, 161 vols. (Paris: 1857–1866)

PL	*Patrologia cursus completus, series Latina*, ed. J.-P. Migne, 217 vols. (Paris: 1841–1855)
StC	*Studia Canonica*
SC	*Sources Chrétiennes* (Paris: Éditions du Cerf, 1955–)
USCCB	United States Conference of Catholic Bishops (since July 1, 2001)

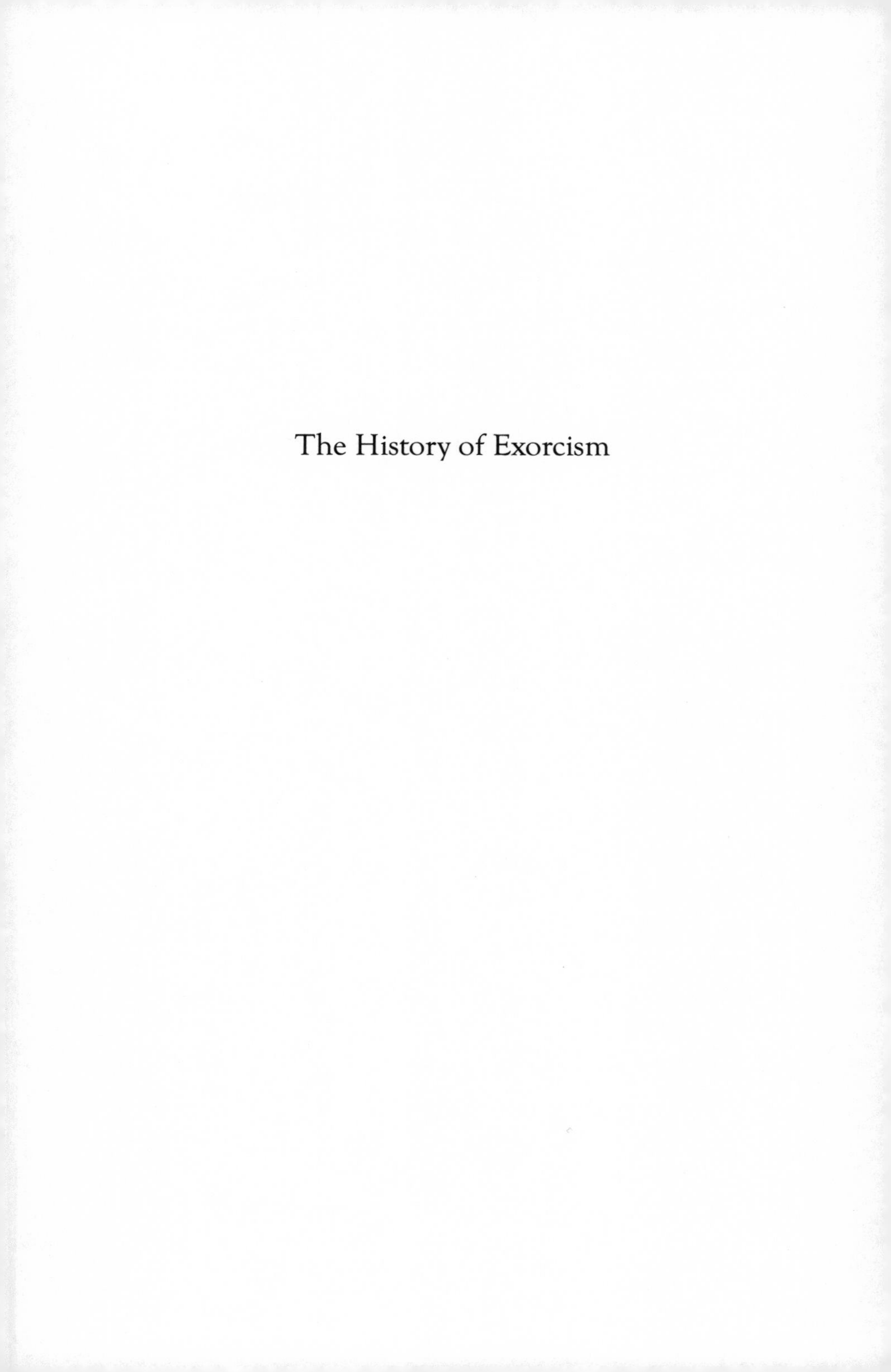

The History of Exorcism

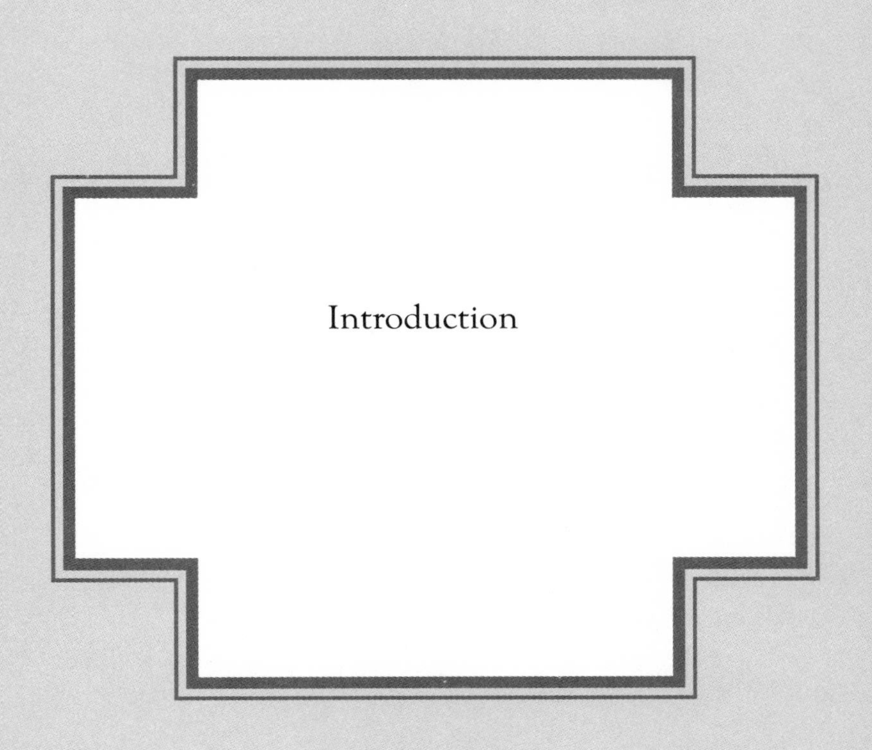

Introduction

+

When we say *exorcism*, we usually refer to the solemn exorcism we have seen in movies and television: a liturgical rite performed by priests intended to drive demons out of a possessed person. Historically, it was not always a fixed liturgical rite, and it was not always performed by priests. In addition to solemn exorcisms there are also exorcistic prayers contained in other liturgical rites that are not solemn exorcisms, such as Baptism and the Rite of Christian Initiation of Adults (RCIA). Finally, there is the "minor" exorcism, written in 1890, intended to free homes, locations, or objects from demonic attachment and manifestation. There are also sacramentals that have exorcistic properties that drive away demons, such as holy water, Church bells, and the St. Benedict medal.

The form of exorcism that has required the most attention in the history of the Church is solemn exorcism. It is the form given the most prominence by Jesus, in action and word. It is also the form most fraught with danger, as it is the circumstance when the Church directly clashes with a demon that is inhabiting a body with which it can strike out, speak, tempt, and manipulate others.

The History of Exorcism

Exorcism has come into a new prominence in Western culture since the 1960s. This is the result of a number of events, as well as tensions within the Church and between the Church and the world. The Church of Satan was founded in 1966, as well as a number of less famous black magic cults. Witchcraft was recreated by Gerald Gardner in the 1960s, spawning the myriad forms of Wicca seen today. Deliverance prayer came to the fore in the Catholic world with the Catholic Charismatic Renewal starting in 1967. William Peter Blatty wrote his book, *The Exorcist*, based on a real case (Robbie Mannheim, exorcised in 1949),[1] in 1971. The movie *The Exorcist*, by William Friedkin, was released in 1973, and it had a huge global impact. Anneliese Michel died after an exorcism in Germany in 1976,[2] and in the same year, Fr. Martin's famous book *Hostage to the Devil* was released worldwide.[3] The "satanic panic" occurred in the 1980s and 1990s in the United States. Fr. Amorth's book *An Exorcist Tells His Story* was released in English in 1999.[4] All of this is not to say that exorcism had entirely left the awareness of the West before the 1960s. There were earlier examples, such as the pamphlet *Begone Satan! A Soul-Stirring Account of Diabolical Possession*, originally published in 1935.[5]

1 T. B. Allen, *Possessed: The True Story of an Exorcism*, 2nd ed. (Lincoln, NE: iUniverse, 2000).

2 F. D. Goodman, *The Exorcism of Anneliese Michel* (Eugene, OR: Resource, 1981).

3 M. Martin, *Hostage to the Devil* (New York: Bantam Books, 1971).

4 G. Amorth, *An Exorcist Tells His Story* (San Francisco: Ignatius Press, 1999).

5 Celestine Kapsner, O.S.B., "Begone Satan!," EWTN, accessed March 10, 2023, https://www.ewtn.com/catholicism/library/begone-satan-6067.

Exorcism as it is portrayed today was actually created in 1614 as part of the Council of Trent (1545–1563). The council was largely a reaction to the Protestant Reformation (1517 onward). The council's particular work on exorcism was a reaction to criticisms of exorcism generally, and criticisms of how it was done in the Middle Ages. There were many exorcism manuals before then, with improvisation and even magic used in some exorcisms. There were also misuses, abuses, and misdiagnoses of possession. In 1703, all versions of exorcism but the 1614 rite, with its strict rules for diagnosing and treating possession, were banned.

Through her whole history, the Church has allowed exorcism to flourish during periods of internal division, and when an outside spiritual enemy is feared.[6] It was often used a proof of the validity of the true Faith, and so historically was sometimes done publicly, or recounted publicly. Demons provide an unambiguous representation of evil. They can easily represent whatever belief, movement, or political force that threatens the Church. Since they are a pure evil that defies all human authority, they were seen to prove which faith is approved by God, since God is presumed to only empower the true Faith. The words spoken by demons, thought to tell the truth in certain circumstances, became "suitable and versatile weapons in inner-church conflicts, theological controversies, and church politics."[7] This reliance on exorcism and the testimony of demons was not a consistent

[6] S. Ferber, *Demonic Possession and Exorcism in Early Modern France* (London: Routledge, 2004), p. 4.

[7] F. D. Goodman, *How about Demons? Possession and Exorcism in the Modern World* (Bloomington, IN: Indiana University Press, 1988), p. 97.

feature of Church history, nor is it a feature today, but it was present in some ages.

Exorcism was common in the early Church when internal arguments about the Faith were many, and an external pagan enemy (Rome) threatened to destroy it. Successful exorcism also served as a proof of holiness for saintly men and women in the early Church (when there was no fixed rite of exorcism, and it was not limited to priests). Exorcisms were used as public tests of which version of the Faith was valid in the Renaissance. There were instances of alternating exorcisms attempted by clergy from Catholic and Protestant Churches. Later, the Second Vatican Council (1962–1965) caused internal division in the Church again, which continues to this day. It is perhaps no accident of history that Western culture and the Church have had a renewed interest in the demonic and exorcism in the years since Vatican II.

In 1968, two American Jesuit scholars, Henry Ansgar Kelly and Juan B. Cortes, argued that exorcism practice should cease on people because theologians had misunderstood the New Testament and misidentified personifications of mental illness as fallen angels.[8] In 1969, Jesuit theologian Herbert Haag published *Goodbye to the Devil*, which argued that the devil was not a spiritual person, but was a relic of the past that the Church had outgrown.[9] Anecdotally, it seems that these views gained favor in the seminaries of the United States. Many priests who went

[8] H. A. Kelly, *Towards the Death of Satan: The Growth and Decline of Christian Demonology* (London: Geoffrey Chapman, 1968). See also H. A. Kelly, *Satan: A Biography* (Cambridge, MA: Cambridge University Press, 2006).

[9] H. Haag, *Abschied vom Teufel*, Theologische Meditationen 23 (New York: Benziger, 1978).

through seminary in the 1970s have reported to the author that they were explicitly told that the devil does not exist, and that possession is only mental illness. On the other side of the issue was a practicing exorcist Jesuit in Germany, Adolf Rodewyk. In 1966, Rodewyk published *Damonische Besessenheiut Heute*, translated to English in 1975 as *Possessed by Satan.*[10] In that book, he reported on many twentieth-century exorcisms. Pope Paul VI partially addressed this internal controversy in his general audience on November 15, 1972:

> We come face to face with sin which is a perversion of human freedom and the profound cause of death because it involves detachment from God, the source of life. And then sin in its turn becomes the occasion and the effect of interference in us and our work by a dark, hostile agent, the Devil. Evil is not merely an absence of something but an active force, a living, spiritual being that is perverted and that perverts others. It is a terrible reality, mysterious and frightening.[11]

In 1975, Fr. Rodewyk consulted on the Anneliese Michel possession case in Germany, and he later testified at the trial of the priests involved. This was a famous case in Europe, where a young lady died of dehydration on July 1, 1976, a few weeks after a long series of exorcisms ended. The trial made audio recordings of the exorcisms public record in Germany, which at

[10] A. Rodewyk, *Possessed by Satan: The Church's Teaching on the Devil, Possession, and Exorcism*, trans. M. Ebon (Garden City, NY: Doubleday, 1975).

[11] Paul VI, General Audience (November 15, 1972), https://www.ewtn.com/catholicism/library/confronting-the-devils-power-8986.

least partially influenced the German bishops to commission an investigation of exorcism ministry in 1979.

In 1967, the Catholic Charismatic Renewal started at Duquesne University in Pittsburgh, quickly spreading throughout the world. Part of the charismatic renewal was an emphasis on the supernatural, including deliverance prayers against evil spirits, which sometimes caused problems. This emphasis on deliverance ministry and praying over people with demonic manifestations spread in both Catholic and Protestant circles over the years.

In 1985, the Congregation for the Doctrine of the Faith issued a corrective letter about deliverance ministry for the world, *Inde ab aliquot annis*.[12] It essentially forbade laypeople from talking with demons, and it required that deliverance ministries be overseen by a priest. Then, in 1992, the International Association of Exorcists was formed in Rome by seven exorcists, which started having meetings to train priests in 1994. Finally, the new rite of exorcism was released on January 26, 1999, in Latin only.[13] The recent history of exorcism, and its implications, can best be seen in the larger context of the Church's whole history with exorcism.

The Church, like in so many other areas, experienced and then tried to resolve the issues inherent in exorcism ministry over the centuries. She saw through her early years that exorcism was

[12] Congregation for the Doctrine of the Faith, Letter *Inde ab aliquot annis* (September 29, 1984), https://www.ewtn.com/catholicism/library/on-the-current-norms-governing-exorcisms-2074.

[13] CDWDS, Decree *De exorcismis et supplicationibus quibusdam, editio typica*, English trans. USCCB, *Exorcisms and Related Supplications* (Washington, DC: ICEL, 2017). Note: this book can only be purchased by bishops in the United States.

a difficult and often dangerous ministry. The law regulating it tightened over time, limiting who could perform an exorcism and under what circumstances, as well as demanding moral certainty about the condition of possession before allowing an exorcism to take place. The wisdom of those centuries was first codified in a succinct way in the *Roman Ritual* of 1614. It was then revisited 385 years later, in 1998, as part of the Vatican II revision of all of the liturgical rites of the Church. The old rite of exorcism was allowed by Pope Benedict in *Summorum pontificum* after the new rite was promulgated. Then Pope Francis limited this freedom by abrogating *Summorum pontificum*, which was interpreted as allowing the free use of the old *Roman Ritual* version of solemn exorcism.

The law regulating exorcism in the Catholic Church has always been an attempt to protect against abuses and the dangers that are inherent in the task of directly interacting with demons using a person's body. There is, however, only one canon currently (c. 1172) that directly addresses exorcism:

> §1. No one can perform exorcisms legitimately upon the possessed unless he has obtained special and express permission from the local ordinary.
>
> §2. The local ordinary is to give this permission only to a presbyter who has piety, knowledge, prudence, and integrity of life.[14]

There are also many helpful directives in the *praenotanda* of the old (1614) and new (1999) exorcism rites. These are

[14] CIC, c. 1172, English trans. by Vatican, https://www.vatican.va/archive/cod-iuris-canonici/eng/documents/cic_lib4-cann1166-1190_en.html.

instructions given to the priest, as well as guidelines and rules based on the experience of centuries.

There are a number of terms for demonic problems that could lead to an exorcism at different points in history. In general, the word *possession* will be used to describe a spiritual problem where demonic spirits trouble a person and can sometimes take over their body and use it as their own for a time. *Oppression* is when demonic spirits trouble a person, can speak in their mind, physically hurt them and affect their body in various other ways. *Infestation* is a spiritual problem where a demonic spirit manifests in a place or near an object in various ways to scare, harm, and generally torment the people there. That place can be land, a building, or the area around the object. Demons were also blamed for medical ailments or psychological problems at various times in history. Exorcisms were sometimes used to treat these, particularly in the Middle Ages, before the diagnosis of possession as separate from medical and mental problems was well developed.

One further point needs to be kept in mind. In early Christian thought, a *demon* was hard to define definitively. Even the issue of whether it was spiritual or physical was debated until the early modern period (1500–1700). The Greek *daimōn* represented a mediator spirit between gods and human beings. The early Christian view was more that it was a mediator between good and evil.[15] There were a plurality of cultures and religious contexts that Christianity spread into, each of which carried

[15] A. K. Petersen, "The Notion of Demon: Open Questions to a Diffuse Concept," in *Die Dämonen*, ed. A. Lange, H. Lichtenberger, and K. F. Diethard Römheld (Tübingen: Mohr Siebeck, 2002), pp. 23–41.

its own assumptions and ideas about spirits. It was only over centuries of theological development and experience with exorcism that the Church came to the clear understanding we have today.

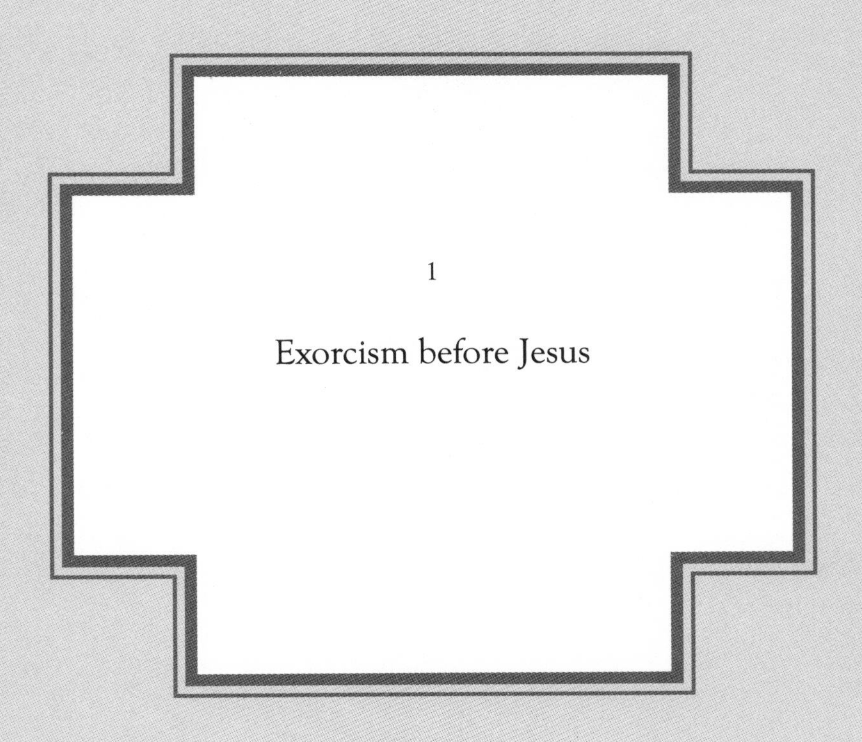

1

Exorcism before Jesus

✢

The Ancient Near East

Since at least the time of the Old Testament (about 1550 BC), the people of the Near East embraced a worldview that included invisible spiritual forces that affect the visible universe.[16] These spiritual forces impacted the day-to-day lives of people, caused illnesses, created good or bad fortune, and ruled over nature.[17] Spiritual forces, such as those determining whether the rains came and food would be available, had to be appeased to ensure survival. The spirits were not seen as inherently good or bad at this early stage of religious development. It was believed that these spirits could be conciliated and befriended through words, actions, and certain materials. The goal was usually purely selfish: to avoid trouble and gain good fortune. The moral character of the person appealing to the spirits was irrelevant at this stage of religion. This type of worldview is called *animism*, and it

[16] E. Langton, *Essentials of Demonology: A Study of Jewish and Christian Doctrine, Its Origins and Development* (Eugene, OR: Wipf and Stock, 2014), p. 11.

[17] Ibid. p. 1.

preceded polytheism, developed into dualism, and finally became monotheism. The magician of animism gave way to the priest of polytheism, where personal moral character started to play a role, and finally to the priest of monotheism, where moral character was central for appealing to the deity in most circumstances.[18]

Many of the religions of the ancient world developed a theology for these spirits, and sometimes developed whole classifications for them.[19] Since people wanted to be free of diseases and mental health problems ascribed to spirits, various religious actions were created to address these problems.[20] Sometimes these actions were intended to ward off disease and misfortune before they happened, and sometimes they were intended to cure a problem that had already set in.[21] Evil spirits and exorcism played prominent roles in the lives of people in the Ancient Near East.[22] Exorcism then was more akin to magic, being based more on the mechanistic repetition of (often nonsense) words, the written word, and symbols.

The Jewish Old Testament Period

The early people of Israel were greatly influenced by the Canaanite religion when they settled with the Caananites in the second

[18] T. Davies, *Magic, Divination, and Demonology among the Hebrews and Their Neighbors* (New York: Ktav, 1969).

[19] A. Finlay, *Demons! The Devil, Possession & Exorcism* (London: Blandford, 1999), p. 11.

[20] T. K. Oesterreich, *Possession and Exorcism among Primitive Races in Antiquity, the Middle Ages, and Modern Times*, trans. D. Ibberson (1922; repr. New York: Causeway Books, 1974), pp. 147–148.

[21] D. Reese, "Demons: New Testament," in *The Anchor Bible Dictionary*, vol. 2 (New York, NY: Doubleday, 1992), p. 140.

[22] Oesterreich, *Possession and Exorcism*, pp. 147–148.

millennium BC.[23] The Canaanite religion of Syria-Palestine included a council of gods led by a high god, *El*, who was the Creator of all things. The early Israelites adopted this idea of a council of gods, but later moved to monotheism. The lasting influence of the Canaanite religion is evidenced in many ways: by El still being used as a byname for Yahweh in the current Hebrew Scriptures, the importance of sacrifices continued from the Canaanite worship of El to the Hebrew temple, and the role of El as a dispenser of kingdoms and lands to peoples continued in the Old Testament.[24] We also see the retention of the suffix -el, designating a spirit which is a son of El, still seen in the names Michael, Gabriel, and Raphael.[25]

The Jews were later influenced by the Assyrian-Babylonian religion during the Babylonian exile (598–538 BC).[26] The Babylonian religion had a more developed set of specific spirit names, functions, and powers. This gave rise to a more concrete and specific list of spiritual workers of misfortune in Jewish demonology.[27] One example is the Babylonian god Lilith. Lilith was incorporated into the Jewish Creation myth as the first wife of Adam who refused to cooperate with God's plan. There is a folk belief to this day that Lilith seeks to kill Jewish male children

[23] Finlay, *Demons!*, p. 14.

[24] T. Mullen, Jr., *The Divine Council in Canaanite and Early Hebrew Literature*, Harvard Semitic Monographs 24 (Chico, CA: Scholars Press, 1980), pp. 1–3.

[25] Mullen, *The Divine Council.* p.15.

[26] L. Boadt, *Reading the Old Testament: An Introduction* (New York, NY: Paulist Press, 1984) pp. 309–311.

[27] J. Morgenstern, art. "Demons," in *The Universal Jewish Encyclopedia,* vol. 3, New York, NY, Universal Jewish Encyclopedia Co., 1948, p. 529.

when they are young, so some traditional Jews allow a boy's hair to grow long until he is three years old. The Jewish hair cutting ceremony is called *upsherin* ("first cutting").

The next influence on Jewish demonology came from the rise of Persian power in the region, which brought the religion of Zoroastrianism. This religion posited a supreme god and a pantheon of lesser good and evil spirits created by that god.[28] A number of these were adopted by the Jewish people and integrated into their cosmology. The idea of Satan was one of these. Their version of Satan was Angra Mainyu, who presided over the forces of evil and opposed Ahura Mazda (their supreme god). This idea of good and bad spirits pitted against each other was new to Jewish cosmology and took the form of angels and demons fighting each other.[29] Azazel, another Zoroastrian evil spirit, is found in Leviticus 16:7–10, where during Yom Kippur a literal scapegoat carries the sins of the people to Azazel. He had been thrown to Earth and trapped under a mountain in the desert as a form of punishment. The goat carried the sins of the people to that mountain and was consumed by Azazel. Azazel has a parallel in the Jewish book of Enoch. There Samyaza, an angel, convinces some other angels to rebel with him and take human wives and teach people forbidden knowledge. They are caught and are cast out of the high heaven, and Samyaza is cast to earth and buried under a mountain.[30] Many of these Zoroastrian themes, and some Canaanite ideas, are detectable in Revelation 12:7–9:

[28] Boadt, *Reading the Old Testament*, p. 50.

[29] Reese, "Demons," in *The Anchor Bible Dictionary*, vol. 2, p. 140.

[30] G. Nickelsburg, *1 Enoch 1: A Critical and Historical Commentary on the Bible* (Minneapolis: Fortress Press, 2001).

> Then war broke out in heaven; Michael and his angels battled against the dragon. The dragon and its angels fought back, but they did not prevail and there was no longer any place for them in heaven. The huge dragon, the ancient serpent, who is called the Devil and Satan, who deceived the whole world, was thrown down to earth, and its angels were thrown down with it.

Up until this point, evil spirits were invisible forces behind disease, madness, bad fortune, and bad weather. There effect was mostly seen as external. There were religious rites to exorcise people and places, but it was to remove these problems, usually not to handle possession of a body by a spirit. An idea closer to modern possession was introduced by the Greeks in 333 BC, when Alexander the Great conquered the region east of the Mediterranean Sea to India. Madness and irrational behavior were seen as the action of a spirit on *and in* the person. These demons could be good or bad in the Greek view, and they could inhabit a human body. They were intermediaries between the physical and the spiritual; they could inspire artistic expression or terrify the mind. This was the Greek idea of a *muse* that inspired actors and artists to be able to create compelling art. This perspective on spiritual afflictions held for the Jews until 166 BC, when they revolted against the Seleucid Empire and Hellenistic influences.[31]

There was then relative peace and stability for about a hundred years. The Jews had developed their theology of monotheism and cosmology with four succeeding influences:

[31] E. Ferguson, *Demonology of the Early Christian World*, Symposium Series 12 (New York, NY: Edwin Mellen Press, 1984), pp. 57–59.

the Canaanite ideas of a single Creator god and set of lesser gods, the Babylonian cast of good and evil spirits who had specific names and functions—as well as ways to ward them off—and the Zoroastrian idea of good and evil spirits at war, with humanity in the crossfire. Finally, there were the Greek ideas of good, bad, and neutral demons inspiring, or potentially inhabiting, people.

In spite of all this influence, we see very little written about demons, their influence on life, or exorcism in the Hebrew Scriptures before the intertestamental period (the time after the Hebrew canon was finalized in about 420 BC, until the Christian Scriptures appeared in the first century AD). There seems to have been a resistance to formally incorporating other cultural views into the Jewish religion. This material was either initially resisted, as proposed by Oesterreich,[32] or it was systematically removed once the Jews were not under direct influence of other cultures for a time, as proposed by Langton.[33] Regardless of the reason, there remain a few references to demons and exorcism in the Old Testament.[34] Satan (which generally means "adversary" or "accuser," and is a Hebrew word that specifically means "to obstruct or oppose") is specifically mentioned only three times.[35]

[32] T. K. Oesterreich, *Possession, Demoniacal and Other: Among Primitive Races, in Antiquity, the Middle Ages, and Modern Times* (New Hyde Park, NY: University Books, 1966), p. 169.

[33] Langton, *Essentials of Demonology*, p. 10.

[34] G. Twelftree, *Christ Triumphant: Exorcism Then and Now* (London: Hodder and Stoughton, 1985), p. 22. The author cites passages from the following books of the Hebrew Scriptures: Leviticus, Numbers, Deuteronomy, 2 Kings, Isaiah, Psalms, and 2 Chronicles.

[35] 1 Chron. 21:1; Job 1 and 2; and Zech. 3:1.

This is enough to at least open the door to the consideration of demons and exorcism as a reality in ancient Judaism.[36]

The oldest example of exorcism in the Bible is found in 1 Samuel 16:14–23, where we find David exorcising Saul by playing the harp. It is important to note the understanding here that evil spirits can only operate with God's awareness and permission, showing the Jewish perspective on God as one sovereign creator over all other spirits:

> The spirit of the Lord had departed from Saul, and he was tormented by an evil spirit from the Lord. So the servants of Saul said to him: "Look! An evil spirit from God is tormenting you. If your lordship will order it, we, your servants here attending to you, will look for a man skilled in playing the harp. When the evil spirit from God comes upon you, he will play and you will feel better." Saul then told his servants, "Find me a good harpist and bring him to me." One of the servants spoke up: "I have observed that a son of Jesse of Bethlehem is a skillful harpist. He is also a brave warrior, an able speaker, and a handsome young man. The Lord is certainly with him."
>
> Accordingly, Saul dispatched messengers to ask Jesse to send him his son David, who was with the flock. Then Jesse took five loaves of bread, a skin of wine, and a young goat, and sent them to Saul with his son David. Thus, David came to Saul and entered his service. Saul became very fond of him and made him his armor-bearer. Saul sent Jesse the message, "Let David stay in my service, for he meets with my approval." Whenever the spirit from

[36] Langton, *Essentials of Demonology*, pp. 52–53.

God came upon Saul, David would take the harp and play, and Saul would be relieved and feel better, for the evil spirit would leave him.

The 150 poetic psalms found in the Bible form the hymnbook of worship songs from ancient Judaism. About half are explicitly attributed to David in the text, some to Solomon, some to Moses, and a few to other authors.[37] Their themes are lament for sin, praise for God, thanksgiving to God, and confidence in God. Psalm 91 holds a special place in Judaism as a psalm of protection and deliverance from evil spirits. The Talmud records opinions calling it the "Song of Evil Spirits" (*Shir Shel Pega'im*).[38] It is the only surviving of the "Four Psalms Against Demons" referenced in the Dead Sea Scroll 11QapocrPs and thought to have been used at exorcisms in Qumran.[39]

You who dwell in the shelter of the Most High,
  who abide in the shade of the Almighty,
Say to the Lord, "My refuge and fortress,
  my God in whom I trust.
He will rescue you from the fowler's snare,
  from the destroying plague,
He will shelter you with his pinions,
  and under his wings you may take refuge;
  his faithfulness is a protecting shield.

[37] See "The Book of Psalms," USCCB, accessed March 8, 2023, https://bible.usccb.org/bible/psalms/0.

[38] Rabbi Nosson Scherman, *The Complete Artscroll Siddur*, 3rd ed. (Brooklyn, NY: Mesorah, 2003).

[39] James VanderKam and Peter Flint, *The Meaning of the Dead Sea Scrolls: Their Significance for Understanding the Bible, Judaism, Jesus, and Christianity* (New York: T and T Clark, 2002), pp.127–128.

You shall not fear the terror of the night
nor the arrow that flies by day,
Nor the pestilence that roams in darkness,
nor the plague that ravages at noon.
Though a thousand fall at your side,
ten thousand at your right hand,
near you it shall not come.
You need simply watch;
the punishment of the wicked you will see.
Because you have the Lord for your refuge
and have made the Most High your stronghold,
No evil shall befall you,
no affliction come near your tent.
For he commands his angels with regard to you,
to guard you wherever you go.
With their hands they shall support you,
lest you strike your foot against a stone.
You can tread upon the asp and the viper,
trample the lion and the dragon.
Because he clings to me I will deliver him;
because he knows my name I will set him on high.
He will call upon me and I will answer;
I will be with him in distress;
I will deliver him and give him honor.
With length of days I will satisfy him,
and fill him with my saving power. (Ps. 91:1–16)

Later affirmations of the importance of Psalm 91 appear. In the Gospel accounts of Jesus' temptation in the desert, the devil challenges Jesus with verses 11–12 of Psalm 91, in Luke 4:9–11:

> Then he led him to Jerusalem, made him stand on the parapet of the temple, and said to him, "If you are the Son of God, throw yourself down from here, for it is written: 'He will command his angels concerning you, to guard you,' and: 'With their hands they will support you, lest you dash your foot against a stone.' "

and in Matthew 4:5–6:

> Then the devil took him to the holy city, and made him stand on the parapet of the temple, and said to him, "If you are the Son of God, throw yourself down. For it is written: 'He will command his angels concerning you' and 'with their hands they will support you, lest you dash your foot against a stone.'"

The Church includes Psalm 91 in the 1614 rite of exorcism (there numbered as Psalm 90),[40] and in the 1998 rite of exorcism.[41] Therefore, while we do not see a well-developed demonology, or a system of exorcism, in the Old Testament period, we do see an acknowledgment of demons, as well as music and at least one song used as an exorcism.

The Intertestamental Period

The Hebrew canon was closed somewhere from 400 BC to 200 BC. In the centuries leading up to the time of Jesus, there were

[40] *Roman Ritual: In Latin and English with Rubrics and Plainchant Notation*, ed. and trans. P. Weller, 3 vols. (Milwaukee, WI: Bruce, 1950–1952), vol. 1, pp. 201.

[41] John Paul II, *The Roman Ritual* (Washington, DC: USCCB, 2017).

two significant developments in Jewish demonology and exorcism. First, a dualistic conflict model developed, pitting God in Heaven with the holy angels against Satan and the fallen angels on Earth. Second, the demon Satan, as a sort of general accuser of people, became personalized into individual demons with particular functions and names.[42]

The books of this period greatly expand the Genesis Creation story, develop the origin, background, powers, and limitations of the demons, and introduce an explanation for the myth of giants in the ancient world. They are apocryphal books and so are outside of Jewish Scripture canon, but they were known to the Jews in the intertestamental period, and at the time of Jesus, and so are important to this topic.

1 Enoch

First Enoch tells the complex story of the fall of the watcher angels (called *Grigori*, or the "sons of God") and the creation of their half-human offspring, called *Nephilim* (described as "men of renown," or "giants" in some translations). The phrase "sons of God" is used in Job 1:6; 2:1; and 38:7 to denote angels. This also denotes the sons of God as "members of the divine council," which harkens back to the Canaanite cosmology covered above.[43] In First Enoch, the presence of these Nephilim offspring, being

[42] D. Hillers, "Demons, Demonology," in *Encyclopedia Judaica*, vol. 5 (Jerusalem: Macmillan, 1971), p. 1525; W. Carr, *Angels and Principalities: The Background, Meaning, and Development of the Pauline Phrase Hai Archai Kai Hai Exousiai* (Cambridge, MA: Cambridge University Press, 1981), p. 42.

[43] See New American Bible note on Job 1:6, "Job, Chapter 1," USCCB, accessed March 8, 2023, https://bible.usccb.org/bible/job/1.

evil, destructive, and outside the plan of creation, led to God sending the flood to destroy them.[44] In the view of First Enoch, the demons, or evil spirits, are the spirits of the giants who were killed by the flood. The watcher angels in this story were locked away in the valleys of the earth for seventy generations.[45] In a parallel to Revelation 12:7–9, Michael is commissioned to imprison Samyaza (this story's parallel for Satan) on Earth. Finally, First Enoch introduces the idea that there is no leniency possible for the evil spirits, even if they plead for it.[46] Some references to this story remain, first in Genesis 6:1–4:

> When human beings began to grow numerous on the earth and daughters were born to them, the sons of God saw how beautiful the daughters of human beings were, and so they took for their wives whomever they pleased. Then the Lord said: My spirit shall not remain in human beings forever, because they are only flesh. Their days shall comprise one hundred and twenty years.
>
> The Nephilim appeared on earth in those days, as well as later, after the sons of God had intercourse with the daughters of human beings, who bore them sons. They were the heroes of old, the men of renown.

Also, in Wisdom 14:6:

> For of old, when the proud giants were being destroyed, the hope of the universe, who took refuge on a raft, left

[44] "Enoch, Books of," in *The Oxford Dictionary of the Christian Church*, 3rd rev. ed., ed. F. Cross and E. Livingstone (Oxford, Oxford University Press, 2005), p. 550.

[45] Nickelsburg, *1 Enoch 1*, p. 215.

[46] Nickelsburg, *1 Enoch 1*, p. 251.

to the world a future for the human family, under the guidance of your hand.

And in Baruch 3:26:

In it were born the giants, renowned at the first, huge in stature, skilled in war.

The interpretation of these Scripture passages in light of 1 Enoch fell out of favor in the early Christian Church. The Sethite interpretation that took its place is best summarized by Julius Africanus (AD 160–240), who popularized it:

The descendants of Seth are called the Sons of God on account of the righteous men and patriarchs who have sprung from him, even down to the Savior Himself; but that the descendants of Cain are named the seed of men, as having nothing divine in them, on account of the wickedness of their race and the inequality of their nature, being a mixed people, and having stirred the indignation of God.[47]

The Book of Giants

The book of Giants was recovered as a set of Aramaic fragments from the Qumran caves. It fills in some of the events during the time when the giant offspring of the evil angels and human women were on the earth. It, like First Enoch, implies that God

[47] Dionysius of Alexandria, *The Extant Fragments of the Five Books of the Chronography of Julius Africanus*, in *Ante-Nicene Fathers*, vol. 6: *Fathers of the Third Century: Gregory Thaumaturgus, Dionysius the Great, Julius Africanus, Anatolius, and Minor Writers, Methodius, Arnobius*, ed. Alexander Roberts, James Donaldson, and A. Cleveland Coxe, trans. S.D.F. Salmond (Buffalo, NY: Christian Literature, 1886), p. 131.

sends the flood in order to exact judgment on the evil angels and their offspring, killing the giants. Before sending the flood, God sends the giants dreams, interpreted for them by Enoch, warning them of a catastrophic end if they do not repent and stop doing evil. The majority of them challenge God to act against them. A battle breaks out between God's angels and the giants, which the giants eventually lose. An interesting literary side note is that the character Humbaba, from the *Epic of Gilgamesh*, appears in the Qumran fragments as one of the giants.

The book of Giants, like First Enoch, warns of the danger of sexual congress between angels and humans. This idea will, many centuries later, impact the idea of incubus and succubus activity by demons in the Middle Ages, and play a role in the witch trials that swept across Europe from 1500 to 1660, and into America from 1647 to 1663.

Tobit

This story, which is Jewish apocrypha, remains in the Catholic and Orthodox Bibles, but was removed from most Protestant Bibles. Sarah had lost seven husbands before she could consummate any of the marriages. The demon Asmodeus (translatable as both "destroyer" and "lustful demon") had not harmed her but killed each of her husbands on their wedding night.[48] It is not clear whether the disembodied Asmodeus had killed them, whether it was Sarah, or whether Sarah was possessed by Asmodeus and killed them under his control. Her maid only states that Sarah has killed them (Tob. 3:8).

Sarah prays that God might let her die, as she feels bad about the seven dead husbands and the reproach of her maid. Instead

[48] Davies, *Magic, Divination, and Demonology*, pp. 101–102.

of letting her die, God sends the angel Raphael to rid her of the demon Asmodeus (Tob. 3:11–17). Raphael does this, but in a roundabout way.

Raphael travels with Tobias to the city of Media, though Tobias does not know Raphael is an angel. Raphael tells him to take the gall, liver, and heart from a large fish. Raphael says that burning the liver and heart causes a smell that drives away demons. When Raphael tells Tobias he should marry Sarah, Tobias is afraid. He says that he has heard of the seven dead husbands, and that a demon was to blame. He says the demon loves her (this love seems to be implied to be of a sexual nature), is jealous, and so kills her husbands. Raphael tells him not to worry (Tob. 6). Later, Tobias burns the liver and heart on embers and the odor causes Asmodeus to flee Sarah and go to the upper desert of Egypt. Raphael pursues Asmodeus and binds him (Tob. 8:1–3).

This story is important for a number of reasons. It introduces a specific demon separate from Satan, Asmodeus. It tells the story of this demon's connection to Sarah, and the deaths he caused. Tobias misunderstands Asmodeus as being a jealous lover of Sarah. This harkens back to the theme in First Enoch of the sons of God finding women beautiful and taking them as wives. Like First Enoch and the book of Giants, it prefigures the Middle Ages idea of demonic sexual attacks, called *incubus* and *succubus* attacks. The power of certain objects and prayer are introduced as effective at driving away demons and keeping them away. Finally, it introduces the idea of holy angels helping mankind in the struggle against the demonic by teaching them things. This parallels the theme of the watchers in First Enoch teaching mankind the forbidden "sciences of Heaven."

Jubilees

The book of Jubilees is an ancient Jewish text of fifty chapters. It is a recapitulation of the book of Genesis, but with the inclusion of the First Enoch story of the evil angels creating the giants, and the subsequent flood that killed them. The idea of sin entering physical creation from union with the evil angels is expanded. Corruption is described as spreading from that contact to all other living flesh on the Earth, leaving nothing good except Noah. The goal of the flood is not exclusively to destroy the giants, but to wipe out all of tainted creation. The focus is on the story after the flood and not the details of the fall of the evil angels.

As Noah and his family are re-populating the earth, the demons are tempting and leading his descendants astray into illness and destruction. These demons are the spirits of the giants who had been killed by the flood. When Noah prays for help, God sends 90 percent of the demons to their judgment in the earth and leaves 10 percent with Mastêma, the leader of the demons. The word *satan* is used, again, as a generic name for any evil spirit that opposes God. Holy angels teach Noah how to make medicines from plants to cure the illnesses caused by the demons. He also learns from them how to make materials that will keep the demons away.[49]

Jubilees reinforces the idea of union between angels and humans as being catastrophic. In this case it leads not only to the creation of the destructive giants, but to a spreading corruption

[49] O. S. Wintermute, "Jubilees," in *The Old Testament Pseudepigrapha: Expansions of the "Old Testament" and Legends, Wisdom and Philosophical Literature, Prayers, Psalms, and Odes, Fragments of Lost Judeo-Hellenistic Works*, vol. 2, ed. J. Charlesworth (Garden City, NY, Doubleday, 1985), p. 47.

of all living things. God is, however, presented as all powerful and in charge of what evil creatures are allowed to do. Finally, prayer is shown as an effective means to control demons.[50]

Jewish Exorcism at the Time of Jesus

We have seen that there was a general belief in good and bad spirits and in exorcism in the Ancient Near East, and specifically among the ancient Jewish people.[51] Leading up to the time of Jesus, belief in possession and exorcism was prevalent among the Jews. Jewish exorcists were known of and operated publicly in society. The nature of their exorcisms is perhaps best conveyed by an eyewitness, the Roman historian Flavius Josephus (AD 37–100):

> And this was the manner of the cure: he [Eleazar] put to the nose of the possessed man a ring which had under its seal one of the roots prescribed by Solomon, and then, as the man smelled it, drew out the demon through his nostrils, and, when the man at once fell down, adjured the demon never to come back into him, speaking Solomon's name and reciting the incantations which he had composed. Then, wishing to convince the bystanders and prove to them that he had this power, Eleazar placed a cup or foot-basin full of water a little way off and commanded the demon, as it went out of the man, to overturn it and make known to the spectators that he had left the man. And when this was done,

[50] Twelftree, *Christ Triumphant*, p. 31.

[51] Davies, *Magic, Divination, and Demonology*, p. 102.

> the understanding and wisdom of Solomon were clearly revealed, on account of which we have been induced to speak of these things.[52]

First, the exorcist makes the demoniac smell a plant root held in a ring he is wearing. This may have some basis in the story from Tobit, where Asmodeus is driven out by the smell of the fish's heart and liver burning. We are also reminded of Noah being taught which plants could be used to ward off demons in the book of Jubilees. It is not clear whether the ring is significant in itself, or whether it was merely a convenient way to hold the root. After the demon is out of the man, the exorcist orders it to not return to him. He invokes the name of Solomon when giving this command. He then recites incantations which he has composed (therefore he was not praying Hebrew Scriptures). Finally, the demon is compelled to put on a preternatural display for the benefit of the onlookers, and the exorcist's reputation (and perhaps his payment). We see that public exorcisms were at least sometimes the norm, and the exorcist was a regular component of society.

[52] Josephus, *Jewish Antiquities*, vol. 5: *Books V–VIII*, trans. H. Thackeray and R. Marcus (Cambridge, MA: Harvard University Press, 1988), 8.2.5, pp. 595–597.

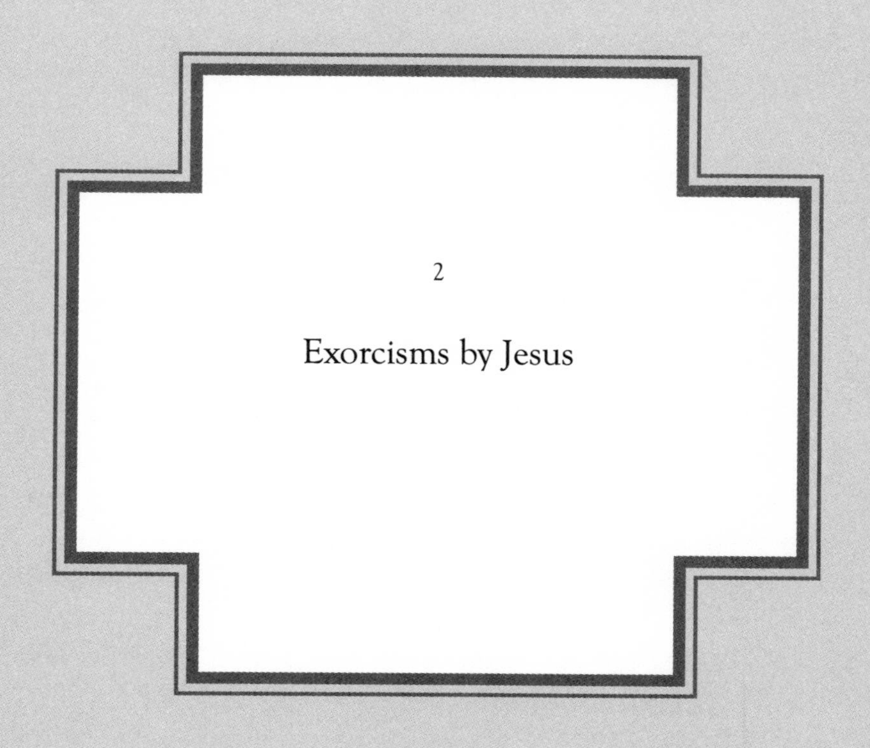

2

Exorcisms by Jesus

✝

Jesus as Exorcist

The Synoptic Gospels present Jesus as a teacher, healer, and exorcist.[53] He was not very unusual in that. There were other charismatic healers and exorcists at the time.[54] There was, however, something very unusual in the way Jesus did exorcisms. We can best see this in His first public miracle in the Gospel of Mark (1:21–28), which started His ministry and created His fame, not because He had exorcised a man, but because of *how He did it:*[55]

> Then they came to Capernaum, and on the sabbath he entered the synagogue and taught. The people were astonished at his teaching, for he taught them as one having authority and not as the scribes. In their synagogue was a

[53] G. Vermès, *Jesus the Jew: A Historian's Reading of the Gospels* (New York, NY: Macmillan, 1973), p. 22.

[54] H. Kee, *Medicine, Miracle, and Magic in New Testament Times*, Society for New Testament Studies 55 (Cambridge, MA: Cambridge University Press, 1986), p. 76.

[55] H. Kee, "The Terminology of Mark's Exorcism Stories," *New Testament Studies* 14 (1967): p. 242.

> man with an unclean spirit; he cried out, "What have you to do with us, Jesus of Nazareth? Have you come to destroy us? I know who you are—the Holy One of God!" Jesus rebuked him and said, "Quiet! Come out of him!" The unclean spirit convulsed him and with a loud cry came out of him. All were amazed and asked one another, "What is this? A new teaching with authority. He commands even the unclean spirits and they obey him." His fame spread everywhere throughout the whole region of Galilee.

The demon in this case seems to have reacted to the presence of Jesus, which initiated the encounter. Here we see no use of roots or smells, no invoking of names, no incantations, no quoting of Scripture, and not even prayer. Jesus simply said, "Come out of him!"

The people were amazed by a few things about this exorcism. First, at the way Jesus did the exorcism: that He had inherent power in Himself alone. Secondly, that the demon recognized His power to destroy them, and said that Jesus was the Holy One of God.[56] Jesus also had no need to tell the demon not to return, and He sought no display for the people; if anything, He told the demon to be quiet.

Later, Jesus entered the territory of the Gerasenes on the eastern shore of the Sea of Galilee. This was a mostly Gentile region inhabited by Greek settlers. The story is in Mark 5:1–20:

> They came to the other side of the sea, to the territory of the Gerasenes. When he got out of the boat, at once a man from the tombs who had an unclean spirit met

[56] G. Twelftree, *Jesus the Exorcist: A Contribution to the Study of the Historical Jesus* (Peabody, MA: Hendrickson, 1993), p. 60.

him. The man had been dwelling among the tombs, and no one could restrain him any longer, even with a chain. In fact, he had frequently been bound with shackles and chains, but the chains had been pulled apart by him and the shackles smashed, and no one was strong enough to subdue him. Night and day among the tombs and on the hillsides he was always crying out and bruising himself with stones. Catching sight of Jesus from a distance, he ran up and prostrated himself before him, crying out in a loud voice, "What have you to do with me, Jesus, Son of the Most High God? I adjure you by God, do not torment me!" (He had been saying to him, "Unclean spirit, come out of the man!") He asked him, "What is your name?" He replied, "Legion is my name. There are many of us. And he pleaded earnestly with him not to drive them away from that territory.

Now a large herd of swine was feeding there on the hillside. And they pleaded with him, "Send us into the swine. Let us enter them." And he let them, and the unclean spirits came out and entered the swine. The herd of about two thousand rushed down a steep bank into the sea, where they were drowned. The swineherds ran away and reported the incident in the town and throughout the countryside. And people came out to see what had happened. As they approached Jesus, they caught sight of the man who had been possessed by Legion, sitting there clothed and in his right mind. And they were seized with fear. Those who witnessed the incident explained to them what had happened to the possessed man and to the swine. Then they began to beg him to leave their district. As he was getting into the boat, the man who had

> been possessed pleaded to remain with him. But he would not permit him but told him instead, "Go home to your family and announce to them all that the Lord in his pity has done for you." Then the man went off and began to proclaim in the Decapolis what Jesus had done for him; and all were amazed.

First, we see some similarities to the synagogue in Capernaum: the demon is agitated by the presence of Jesus, and it identifies Jesus' true nature. We also see a critical difference: Jesus had been telling the demon to come out, but the demon seems to have resisted, and said, "I adjure you by God, do not torment me!" Jesus then asks the demon's name, a critical addition to the exorcism. Within the Jewish understanding, to surrender your name *is the same as surrendering yourself.*[57] Jesus, as God, already knew the name of the demon and had complete power over it; the critical action was the demon being forced to openly surrender that power to Jesus. That was a sign of submission.[58] The final action, Jesus allowing them to enter the swine, was not unheard of. The idea that demons could be transferred from a person to another object was not unusual to the Jews at the time.[59]

It was not unusual for exorcists of the time to exorcise people from a distance.[60] In Mark 7:24–30, we see Jesus responding to a Gentile mother of a daughter who was possessed:

> From that place he went off to the district of Tyre. He entered a house and wanted no one to know about it, but he

[57] H. Van Der Loos, *The Miracles of Jesus* (Leiden: E.J. Brill, 1965), p. 388.

[58] Twelftree, *Jesus the Exorcist*, p. 84.

[59] Langton, *Essentials of Demonology*, p. 158.

[60] Twelftree, *Jesus the Exorcist*, p. 146.

> could not escape notice. Soon a woman whose daughter had an unclean spirit heard about him. She came and fell at his feet. The woman was a Greek, a Syrophoenician by birth, and she begged him to drive the demon out of her daughter. He said to her, "Let the children be fed first. For it is not right to take the food of the children and throw it to the dogs." She replied and said to him, "Lord, even the dogs under the table eat the children's scraps." Then he said to her, "For saying this, you may go. The demon has gone out of your daughter." When the woman went home, she found the child lying in bed and the demon gone.

In this instance, Jesus models the power of prayer, in this case directed to him, to liberate people. No apparent action is needed at all in this case: Jesus merely tells her that it is already done. Clearly, this is an even greater departure from the normative model of exorcism at the time.

Finally, we consider the case of the epileptic boy in Mark 9:17–29, which contains new insights into Jesus' exorcisms:

> Someone from the crowd answered him, "Teacher, I have brought to you my son possessed by a mute spirit. Wherever it seizes him, it throws him down; he foams at the mouth, grinds his teeth, and becomes rigid. I asked your disciples to drive it out, but they were unable to do so." He said to them in reply, "O faithless generation, how long will I be with you? How long will I endure you? Bring him to me." They brought the boy to him. And when he saw him, the spirit immediately threw the boy into convulsions. As he fell to the ground, he began to roll around and foam at the mouth. Then he questioned his father, "How long has this been happening to him?"

> He replied, "Since childhood. It has often thrown him into fire and into water to kill him. But if you can do anything, have compassion on us and help us." Jesus said to him, "'If you can!' Everything is possible to one who has faith." Then the boy's father cried out, "I do believe, help my unbelief!" Jesus, on seeing a crowd rapidly gathering, rebuked the unclean spirit and said to it, "Mute and deaf spirit, I command you: come out of him and never enter him again!" Shouting and throwing the boy into convulsions, it came out. He became like a corpse, which caused many to say, "He is dead!" But Jesus took him by the hand, raised him, and he stood up. When he entered the house, his disciples asked him in private, "Why could we not drive it out?" He said to them, "This kind can only come out through prayer."

Jesus' disciples were unable to drive this demon out. Jesus then complains of a lack of faith, but it is not yet clear if it is on the part of the father or His disciples. When the boy is presented to Jesus the father asks if Jesus can do anything, and then we see that Jesus was referring to the father. The father then prays, "I do believe, help my unbelief!" Jesus seems to accept this as adequate on the father's part, so He casts the demon out. Later, when Jesus was with His disciples in private, they asked Him why they could not cast it out. Strangely, He does not reference the father's lack of faith, but their lack of prayer. The variant for this final line is "This kind can only come out through prayer and through fasting."[61]

[61] See New American Bible note on Mark 9:29, "Mark, Chapter 9," USCCB, accessed March 8, 2023, https://bible.usccb.org/bible/mark/9.

Here, we see Jesus teaching the people about the importance of faith, and His disciples about the importance of prayer and fasting, in exorcism. Jesus needs nothing, and in the case of the woman's daughter, need do nothing at all to perform exorcisms. The people and His disciples need to rely on their faith and relationship with God, which is strengthened through prayer and fasting.

The exorcisms of Jesus had new and unprecedented features that the Jewish authorities could not accept. The scribes concluded that His apparent power had to come from Him being in league with Beelzebul, the ruler of the demons. In Luke 11:19–20, Jesus made a critical proclamation about both Himself and the meaning of His exorcistic work:

> If I, then, drive out demons by Beelzebul, by whom do your own people drive them out? Therefore they will be your judges. But if it is by the finger of God that [I] drive out demons, then the kingdom of God has come upon you.

Jesus claimed that His exorcisms were manifestations of the Kingdom of God, and were "nothing less than the cosmic plan of God by which he was regaining control over an estranged and hostile creation, which was under subjection to the powers of Satan."[62]

The Empowering and Commissioning of the Church

Jesus performed many exorcisms as part of His public ministry. These were signs of His divine power, as He had, in himself,

[62] Kee, "The Terminology of Mark's Exorcism Stories," p. 246.

full power over demons. He had no need of any object, name, incantation, or prayer, like the other exorcists of His time.

Jesus also explicitly empowered His twelve disciples with authority over demons in all of the Synoptic Gospels:

> Then he summoned his twelve disciples and gave them authority over unclean spirits to drive them out and to cure every disease and every illness. (Matt. 10:1)

> He summoned the Twelve and began to send them out two by two and gave them authority over unclean spirits. (Mark 6:7)

> He summoned the Twelve and gave them power and authority over all demons and to cure diseases. (Luke 9:1)

Finally, when Jesus commissioned His twelve disciples to go and do their work, He explicitly included the exercise of that authority over demons:

> As you go, make this proclamation: "The kingdom of heaven is at hand." Cure the sick, raise the dead, cleanse lepers, drive out demons. (Matt. 10:7–8)

Many Protestant Christians claim that Jesus gave power over demons to *all* Christians based on Luke 10:17–20:

> The seventy[-two] returned rejoicing, and said, "Lord, even the demons are subject to us because of your name." Jesus said, "I have observed Satan fall like lightning from the sky. Behold, I have given you the power 'to tread upon serpents' and scorpions and upon the full force of the enemy and nothing will harm you. Nevertheless, do not rejoice because the spirits are subject to you, but rejoice because your names are written in heaven."

Whether all Christians, some Christians, or only priests and bishops have authority to cast out demons would be revealed in time. Many centuries of experience would give the Church the wisdom to limit the exercise of the sacramental of exorcism and codify that limit into law. We now turn to that development.

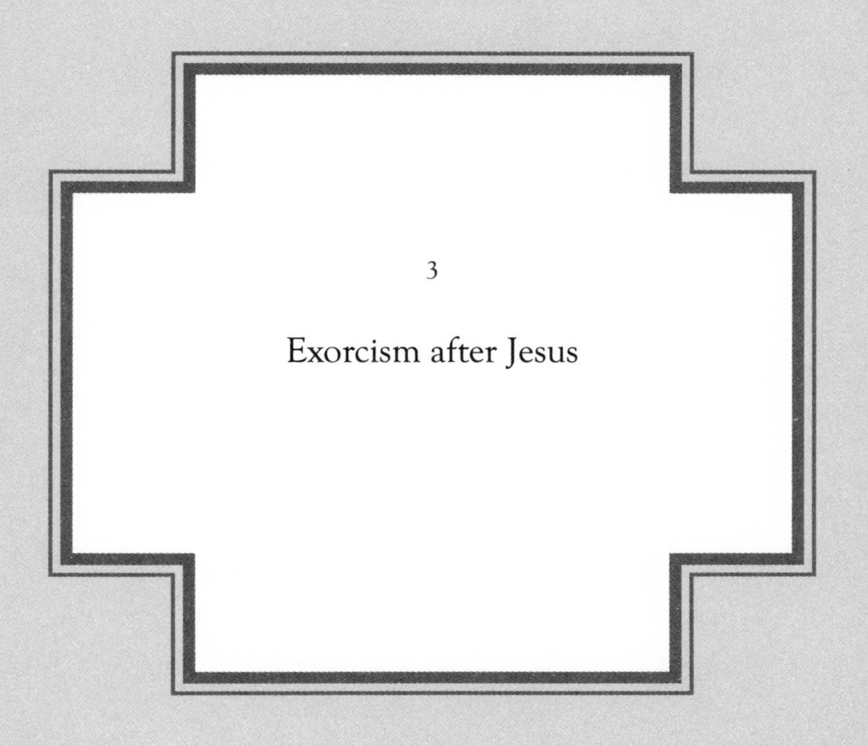

3

Exorcism after Jesus

✝

Exorcisms of the Apostles

After the Resurrection of Jesus and the imparting of the Holy Spirit at Pentecost, the apostles started performing many signs that stood as proofs of the truth of their preaching. Immediately after Pentecost, we read of many people being delivered from unclean spirits in Jerusalem:

> A large number of people from the towns in the vicinity of Jerusalem also gathered, bringing the sick and those disturbed by unclean spirits, and they were all cured. (Acts 5:16)

Philip is specifically described as exorcising many people in Samaria after the apostles went out to preach in different cities:

> Thus Philip went down to [the] city of Samaria and proclaimed the Messiah to them. With one accord, the crowds paid attention to what was said by Philip when they heard it and saw the signs he was doing. For unclean spirits, crying out in a loud voice, came out of

> many possessed people, and many paralyzed and crippled people were cured. There was great joy in that city. (Acts 8:5–8)

The first detailed exorcism account is of Paul exorcising a soothsaying girl in Philippi:

> As we were going to the place of prayer, we met a slave girl with an oracular spirit, who used to bring a large profit to her owners through her fortune-telling. She began to follow Paul and us, shouting, "These people are slaves of the Most High God, who proclaim to you a way of salvation." She did this for many days. Paul became annoyed, turned, and said to the spirit, "I command you in the name of Jesus Christ to come out of her." Then it came out at that moment. (Acts 16:16–18)

Here we see two details familiar from Jesus' exorcisms: the demon recognizes Paul and Silas, and it proclaims this to the witnesses. Then Paul casts the demon out, but does so in the name of Jesus instead of claiming his own authority. This is a critical difference between Jesus and His Christian followers. Even though Jesus gave them authority over demons (Matt 10:1; Mark 6:7; and Luke 9:1, quoted above), Paul still invoked the authority of Jesus' name. The implications of this are even stronger when we consider that Paul is not just any Christian. He is an apostle, a celibate, an ascetic, and wholly devoted to prayer and the gospel, who wrote about a third of the New Testament. If Paul had to rely on the name of Jesus, it seems a clear statement that all Christians must. An important additional aspect of this is that it takes the focus off of Paul and puts it in its proper place: on Jesus Christ.

Exorcism in the Period of Roman Persecution, 0–313

The Roman Empire persecuted Christians during a number of periods in the first three centuries of the Church. This persecution was mainly because Christianity opposed the pagan religion of Rome, and Christians usually refused to give honor to Roman gods or emperors (who were sometimes deified as gods). This occurred first as local persecutions under Nero (54–68), Marcus Aurelius (161–180), Decius (249–251), Trebonianus Gallus (251–260), and Shapur I (240–270). Gallienus (253–268) halted the local persecutions. Then Augustus Diocletian (283–305) instituted a general persecution of the Christians across the empire, which continued until the Edict of Serdica in 311. The Romans had tolerated Judaism and their refusal to honor Roman gods because of their long-established history. The Romans respected ancient religions, but the Christians were brand new.

In spite of these persecutions, the Church grew in popularity over these centuries. The many martyrs who died instead of renouncing their faith or honoring pagan gods became an important source of strength and courage to others. The martyrs also contributed to the idea of honoring Christians who had lived exemplary lives, the saints. A *saint* is simply a person whom we are confident is in Heaven, and so can pray for us in a particularly effective way.

There were two types of exorcisms performed: pre-baptismal exorcism for pagans entering the Church, and exorcism of possessed people. The exorcisms for pagans entering the Church were to remove the influence of the devil (worshipped under the guise of pagan gods), not to relieve demonic possession. There were also instances of possessed people seeking to enter the Church, who needed both. The people that did the pre-baptismal exorcisms were generally different than those that prayed for possessed people. Those who prayed for possessed people were usually groups of the lay faithful who had a charism for exorcism. These lay people were held in high regard during these centuries. The office of priesthood grew slowly over this period, with apostles being regarded as priests, then priests and deacons being ordained to do some of the work for the apostles as the Church grew larger.

Justin Martyr (AD 100–165) makes a reference to Christian exorcists in his *Second Apology*:

> For throughout the whole world and in your own city many of us, human beings who are Christians, exorcised many who were possessed by demons in the name of Jesus Christ who was crucified under Pontius Pilate. And they healed them, though they had not been healed by all the others—exorcists and enchanters and sorcerers. And still they heal, breaking the power of the demons and chasing them away from human beings who were possessed by them.[63]

In this, and other writings, Justin Martyr emphasizes the name of Jesus Christ as being the source of power in Christian exorcisms. He does not reveal any specifics about who exactly is doing exorcisms, except that they are many of the Christians.

Tertullian (AD 160–220) gives more detail about Christian exorcisms in his *Apologeticum*:

[63] Justin Martyr, *Second Apology*, 5.6, in *Justin, Philosopher and Martyr: Apologies*, ed. H. Chadwick, trans. D. Minns and P. Parvis, Oxford Early Christian Texts (Oxford: Oxford University Press, 2009), p. 289.

> Our domination and power over them are possible from the naming of Christ and from their memory of those threatening things that they are expecting from God through Christ the judge: fearing Christ in God and God in Christ, they are subjected to the servants of God and of Christ. Thus from our touch and breath, with the contemplation and realization of their punishment of fire, and by our command, they depart from bodies, unwilling and sorrowing and ashamed before you who are present.[64]

In both of these citations from the early Church, we do not see qualifiers used about which Christians can exorcise demons. Tertullian seems to contend that every Christian received the power to cast out demons when they were baptized. We need to note two facts, however: these documents were written for pagans in order to extol the validity of Christianity and not to define internal Church law, and secondly, neither say *all* Christians performed exorcisms, just that some Christians did. We do find some additional clarity on this point from Irenaeus, in his treatise *Against Heresies*:

> Wherefore his true disciples, receiving grace from him, perform such works in his name for the benefit of other men, as each has received the gift from him. For some of them drive out demons effectually and truly, so that those who have been cleansed from evil spirits frequently believe and unite with the Church. Others have a foreknowledge of future events, and visions, and prophetic revelations. Still others heal the sick by the laying on of hands, and restore

[64] Tertullian, *Apologeticum*, 23.15–16 (*Corpus Christianorum, Series Latina* 1:132–22).

> them to health. And, as we have said, even dead persons have been raised, and remained with us many years.[65]

For Irenaeus, the power to exorcise demons is one of the charismatic gifts, like healing or prophecy, that are given to *some* in the Christian community.

Origen (AD 185–253) emphasizes two points about exorcism in his writing: the great power in the name of Jesus, and that exorcism does not require high intellect and education:

> For they do not *get the power which they seem to possess* by any *incantations* but by the name of Jesus with the recital of the histories about him. For when these are pronounced they have often made daemons to be driven out of men, and especially when those who utter them speak with real sincerity and genuine belief. In fact the name of Jesus is so powerful against daemons that sometimes it is effective even when pronounced by bad men. It is clear that Christians make no use of spells, but only of the name of Jesus with other words which are believed to be effective taken from the divine scripture.[66]

> Without any curious magical art or sorcerer's device, but with prayer alone and very simple adjurations and formulas such as the simplest person could use. For generally speaking it is uneducated people who do this kind of work.[67]

[65] Irenaeus of Lyon, *Five Books Against Heresies*, W. Harvey (ed.), Rochester, St. Irenaeus Press, 2013.

[66] Origen, *Contra Celsum*, 1.6, in *Origen: Contra Celsum*, trans. H. Chadwick (Cambridge, MA: Cambridge University Press, 1980), pp. 9–10 (*SC*, vol. 132, pp. 90–92).

[67] Origen, *Contra Celsum*, 7.4, in *Origen: Contra Celsum*, pp. 397–398 (*SC*, vol. 150, p. 22).

Origen is trying to differentiate Christian exorcism from pagan exorcism practices, which were seen as magic. For the Christian, power comes from Jesus and not the individual Christian. The individual contributes "sincerity and genuine belief," but nothing more. To emphasize that sole power is in Jesus, he says that complex learning and memorization are not needed, as seems to be the case for the pagan exorcists, who used complex incantations.

Cyprian of Carthage (AD 210–258) makes the first reference to exorcists as a category of the faithful in his letter to Januarius and other Numidian bishops about baptizing heretics:

> Through the exorcists (*exorcistas*), by the human voice and divine power the devil is scourged, scorched, and tormented, and although he may often say that he is departing and leaving the men of God, he lies in what he says, and that which he effected long ago through Pharaoh he perpetrates with the same stubborn and fraudulent guile. But when one comes to the saving water and the sanctification of baptism, we ought to know and believe that the devil is there overpowered and that the man dedicated to God is freed by divine mercy.[68]

The exorcists Cyprian mentions here were members of the clergy specifically appointed to minister to the possessed.[69] This letter also introduces the idea of exorcism linked to Baptism, as opposed to exorcism of the possessed outside of Baptism. At

[68] Cyprian, *Epistula* 69, 15.2 (*CSEL*, vol. 3.2, p. 764).

[69] D. G. Van Slyke, "The Order of Exorcist among the Latin Fathers Reconsidered in the Light of Martin of Tours," *Ephemerides Liturgicae* 123 (2009): pp. 367–375.

that time in Carthage exorcism played a role in preparing some of the people for Baptism.[70]

Pope Gaius (AD 282–295) formally established the orders of the Church as porter, lector, exorcist, subdeacon, deacon, presbyter (priest), and finally bishop.[71] So, by the mid-third century, the function of exorcism was restricted to an order of clergy within the Church. It went from being a charism in lay people to an office of the Church.

Lucius Caecilius Firmianus (AD 250–325), called Lactantius, was a Christian who lived under the persecution of Rome for most of his life. He became an advisor to Emperor Constantine I (303-337), and guided much of the Christian religious policy after Rome legalized Christianity in 313. Constantine I was the first Roman Emperor to convert to Christianity. His mother, Helena, was a Christian and influenced him in his youth. He formally converted in 312, and the Christian religion became the state religion of the Roman Empire at that time. Lactantius believed that the persecutions by the Romans was due to them being possessed by demons:

> The men themselves do not persecute, who do not have a reason why they should be angry with the innocent; but those unclean, abandoned spirits to whom the truth is both known and unwanted, insinuate themselves into their minds and incite them, unwitting, to fury.[72]

70 Van Slyke, "The Order of Exorcist among the Latin Fathers," p. 359.

71 *Liber pontificalis*, 29, in *Gestorum pontificum Romanorum*, vol. 1.1, ed. Theodor Mommsen (Leipzig: Weidmann, 1898).

72 Lactantius, *Divine Institutes*, Translated by A. Bowne and P. Garnsey, Liverpool, Liverpool University Press, 2004.

Lactantius wrote about four themes of possession and exorcism at that time in Rome. These themes have basically continued through the history of exorcism to this day. They are:

1. Possession is a sign of division among Christians, theological or political. Lactantius believed that possession would not occur in harmonious Christian communities.
2. Successful exorcism is an indicator of God's approval of the religion doing the exorcism, and of the person doing the exorcism. Exorcism vindicates the truth.
3. There is power in the name of God, even when used by bad people.
4. Violence, physical or spiritual, is part of the process of exorcism. The physical violence is toward the person doing the exorcism.[73]

We also have an indication that starting in the third century, the Church required that physical objects destined for use in sacraments had to be exorcised. The objects needed to be free from demons in order to become purely God's creatures. This is likely where the terms "creature of oil," "creature of salt," and so forth came from in the early Church.[74] There was an early understanding that to bring an object into its original state as purely a creature of God made it unnecessary to bless it, as it was now in a holy state by its very nature. Kelly has

[73] The author, having assisted at over a thousand exorcisms, can attest to this. He has been punched, kicked, gouged with nails, bitten, choked, wrestled with, and spit upon hundreds of times. Verbal violence has been even more extensive.

[74] A. A. R. Bastiaensen, "Exorcism: Tackling the Devil by Word of Mouth," *Vos and Otten* (2011): p. 136.

argued that, at least in the case of the Stowe Missal of Ireland, that the older exorcism of water was clumsily combined with a newer rite of blessing.[75]

There is a development of the blessing of water through the various Roman rituals, in which we see these same components of the blessing: exorcising it to make it pure, and then blessing it. In addition, we see particular properties of the blessing, specific effects that are asked of God. These effects make the sacramental not only blessed, but also make it a weapon against the demonic. This makes it specifically helpful in both formal exorcism rites of the Church, but also to the lay faithful, who may use it in their private lives. The unofficial English translation of the blessing for water in the commonly available Weller translation of the pre-Vatican II *Roman Ritual* is a good example:

> V. Our help is in the name of the Lord.
> R. Who made heaven and earth.
>
> EXORCISM OF SALT
>
> O salt, creature of God, I exorcise you by the living God, by the true God, by the holy God, by the God who ordered you to be poured into the water by Eliseus the Prophet so that its life-giving powers might be restored. I exorcise you so that you may become a means of salvation for believers, that you may bring health of soul and body to all who make use of you, and that you may put to flight and drive away from the places where you are sprinkled every apparition, villainy, and turn of devilish deceit, and

[75] H.A. Kelly, *The Devil at Baptism: Ritual, Theology and Drama* (Ithaca, NY: Cornell University Press, 1985), pp. 226–227.

every unclean spirit, adjured by Him Who will come to judge the living and the dead and the world by fire.
R. Amen.

Let us pray.
Almighty and everlasting God, we humbly implore Thee, in Thy immeasurable kindness and love, to bless † and sanctify † this salt which Thou did create and give over to the use of mankind, so that it may become a source of health for the minds and bodies of all who make use of it, and may rid whatever it touches or sprinkles of all uncleanness and protect it from every assault of evil spirits. Through our Lord, Jesus Christ, Thy Son, Who lives and reigns with Thee in the unity of the Holy Spirit, God, for ever and ever.
R. Amen.

Exorcism of Water

O water, creature of God, I exorcise you in the name of God the Father almighty, and in the name of Jesus Christ His Son, our Lord, and in the power of the Holy Spirit. I exorcise you so that you may put to flight all the power of the Enemy, and be able to root out and supplant that Enemy with his apostate angels: through the power of our Lord Jesus Christ, Who will come to judge the living and the dead and the world by fire.
R. Amen.

Let us pray.
O God, Who for the salvation of mankind has built Thy greatest mysteries on this substance, water, in Thy kindness hear our prayers and pour down the power of Thy

blessing † into this element, made ready for many kinds of purifications. May this, Thy creature, become an agent of divine grace in the service of Thy mysteries, to drive away evil spirits and dispel sickness, so that every-thing in the homes and other buildings of the faithful that is sprinkled with this water may be rid of all uncleanness and freed from every harm. Let no breath of infection, no disease-bearing air, remain in these places. May the wiles of the lurking Enemy prove of no avail. Let whatever might menace the safety and peace of those who live here be put to flight by the sprinkling of this water, so that the healthfulness, obtained by calling upon Thy holy name, may be made secure against all attack. Through our Lord Jesus Christ, Thy Son, Who lives and reigns with Thee in the unity of the Holy Spirit, God, for ever and ever.
R. Amen.

(The priest mixes a little salt into the water.)

May a mixture of salt and water now be made in the name of the Father †, and of the Son †, and of the Holy Spirit †.
R. Amen.

V. The Lord be with you.
R. And with your spirit.

Let us pray.

Similar exorcistic properties can be found in most of the pre-Vatican II blessings of the Church. The church bell is given the property to drive demons away from the parish when tolled, and to keep people from distraction at Mass. The religious habit is given the property of defending the wearer against the temptations of the demons. The crucifix is given manifold properties, including driving away the demons from anyone who devoutly prays before it. When taken as a whole, it can be seen that almost everything the Church sanctifies with blessings is part of the spiritual warfare that the Body of Christ wages against the kingdom of the prince of this world. Exorcism was an important component of early Christianity, and while it was known in other religions, it became most prominent in Christianity in these various ways, and even helped define it. Even at this early period, and through most of her history, exorcism played an integral role in almost all of the Church.

A complication of possession and exorcism in this early period is that some believed that possession by God, angels, or dead saints was possible.[76] This was a kind of divine possession. Possession was not always considered a bad thing in this sense, but a neutral phenomenon until its nature was determined. This idea, that possession can have a mystical character (a personal direct connection to God or a heavenly spirit), as opposed to demonic, resurfaced in the late medieval and early modern approach to exorcism.[77] Part of the diagnosis then was whether this was a good or a bad spirit possessing the person.[78] Possession was also sometimes linked to prophecy, where a divine spirit

[76] D. Frankfurter, "Where the Spirits Dwell: Possession, Christianization, and Saints' Shrines in Late Antiquity," *Harvard Theological Review* 103, no. 1 (January 2010): pp. 27–46.

[77] N. Caciola, *Discerning Spirits: Divine and Demonic Possession in the Middle Ages* (Ithaca, NY: Cornell University Press, 2003).

[78] G. Ericson, "The Enigmatic Metamorphosis: From Divine Possession to Demonic Possession," *Journal of Popular Culture* 11, no. 3 (Winter 1977): pp. 656–681.

spoke through the person, or even when demons were supposedly compelled to testify to the truth of something. This early openness to possession by good spirits, and relying on demonic testimony, has fallen out of favor since 1614.[79]

Exorcism in the Early Church of the West, 313–900

The Church became more complex and organized as she became a powerful institution of the Roman Empire. She was now not only free of interference, but she had powerful backing. There were developments in the way the Church thought about various issues, dogmas were defined, and heretical ideas were condemned. The dramatic pre-baptismal exorcisms were reinterpreted in non-exorcistic terms by Augustine and others. In 386, Augustine gives us his definition of the exorcism of possessed people outside of Baptism:

> An extrinsic unclean spirit invades the soul and disturbs the senses, and brings fury into certain men; those who take charge of shutting him out are said to lay on hands or exorcize, that is to expel him by adjuring the divine [name].[80]

The exorcism of demoniacs outside of baptismal rites was gradually transformed from being a non-liturgical lay ministry to a rarer miracle that only especially holy people (living saints),

[79] We can see modern exploitation of this old idea, as some people hold themselves out to be mediums, or channelers, of good spirits. Usually this takes the form of necromancy, but it also takes the form of false prophecy.

[80] Augustine, *De Beata Vita*, 3 (*PL*, vol. 32: p. 968).

living or dead, could perform. These people were usually famous for holiness or other miracles, and their stories of exorcism were shared as proofs of the Faith. *Traditio Apostolica*, the book that defined Church rules in Rome in 235, prohibited anyone who had received the spiritual gift of doing exorcisms from being ordained a priest.[81] This clearly separated pre-baptismal exorcisms, done by priests and bishops, from exorcisms of possessed people, which were done by gifted laypeople who could never be priests. This was affirmed in 375–380 by *Constitutiones Apostolorum*, a collection of eight books attributed to the apostles that defined worship, doctrine, and discipline in the Church. It said that exorcists were not to be ordained, because their success depends on their personal characteristics and gifts.[82] This was in contrast to the action of God in response to priestly acts, which does not depend on the priest's personal faith and integrity, but depends on the Church and God. *Traditio Apostolica* also recognized that pre-baptismal exorcisms were not adequate for treating possessed people. It specified that a candidate for Baptism who was possessed must first go and be exorcised separately from the pre-baptismal rite.[83]

Unfortunately, there are no surviving examples of exorcism rites for possessed people from about the first five centuries of the Church.[84] We do know that exorcisms involved a long and

[81] Hippolytus of Rome, *Traditio Apostolica*, in *La Tradition Apostolique*, ed. B. Botte (Paris: Éditions du Cerf, 1946), 15, p. 43.

[82] *Constitutiones Apostolorum*, ed. P.A. Lagarde (London: Williams and Norgate, 1862), 8.25–26, p. 265.

[83] Hippolytus of Rome, *Traditio Apostolica*, in *La Tradition Apostolique*, 16, p. 44.

[84] F. Young, *A History of Exorcism in Catholic Christianity*, Palgrave Historical Studies in Witchcraft and Magic (London: Palgrave Macmillan, 2016), pp. 8–9.

drawn-out process. The *Statuta Ecclesiae Antiqua*, a fifth-century collection of Church decrees, says that "the exorcists should lay their hands on the energumens every day." *Energumen* was a term created in the fourth century to denote people possessed by demons, as opposed to unbelievers who had not yet been baptized. It also says that "the energumens should sweep the floors of the houses of God" and they should be exorcised every day at an opportune time.[85] Having possessed people live in the Church and help with daily tasks indicates that exorcism was a long process, which is what is seen today. The criticism of modern exorcism as being defective because of the length of the cases is therefore likely invalid. Finally, Augustine noted that unclean spirits claimed that the words and actions of the extra-baptismal exorcists caused them the pain of burning.[86]

In addition to the prayers of a gifted layperson, a dead holy person could sometimes exorcise a possessed person brought to their tomb.[87] Usually, the saint would appear in a dream and free the person. This idea was extended to taking part of the tomb, or body, out to possessed people in other places. This effect of these relics, in addition to physical healing miracles, greatly contributed to the practice of using relics of saints as sources of spiritual power and healing. In addition, the idea of exorcised and blessed salt, oil, and water were developed during this time. All of this helped lay the foundation for the medieval exorcism practice which would be developed later.

[85] *Statuta Ecclesiae Antiqua* (*Concilia Galliae*), ed. C. Munier and C. De Clerq (Turnhout: Brepols, 1963), 62–64, p. 176.

[86] Augustine, *Ennarationes in Psalmos*, 65.17 (*PL*, vol. 36: p. 797).

[87] Young, *A History of Exorcism in Catholic Christianity*, pp. 54–55, 90, 97.

Athanasius of Alexandria (AD 296–373) emphasized the need for simplicity in early Christian exorcism practice. In his *Letter to Marcellinus*, he tells how exorcists who used long incantations were mocked by the demons for doing so.[88] In *On the Incarnation*, he contends that the power of the Sign of the Cross is sufficient to drive away demons.[89]

Epiphanius (AD 315–403) also emphasized simplicity in exorcism. In his *Refutation of All the Heresies* (*Panarion*) he gives the three elements of an exorcism: blessing of water, sprinkling the possessed with it, and invoking the name of Jesus.[90]

In the fourth century, there was a general increase in writings about saints performing exorcisms. These were not formal exorcism rites of the Church, but usually ad hoc exorcisms created in the moment. The stories of these exorcisms were not intended for the pagans, but to increase a devotion to the cult of the saints in the faithful.[91] These saints were not necessarily ordained exorcists, and the methods they used often did not involve a command to depart, but a prayer to Jesus to free the person. This is an early example of the difference between exorcistic prayer (commands) and deliverance prayer (usually a

[88] Athanasius, *Letter to Marcellinus*, 33; Athanasius, *The Life of Antony and the Letter to Marcellinus*, trans. R. Gregg (New York, NY: Paulist Press, 1980), pp. 128–129.

[89] Athanasius, *On the Incarnation*, 47; Athanasius, *Contra Gentes and De Incarnatione*, trans. R. Thomson (Oxford: Clarendon Press, 1971), p. 253 (*PG*, vol. 25, pp. 177–180).

[90] *The Gospel of the Ebionites*, 30.10.4–7; Epiphanius, *The Panarion of St. Epiphanius, Bishop of Salamis*, trans. P. Amidon (Oxford, Oxford University Press, 1990), pp. 99–100.

[91] D. G. Van Slyke, "The Human Agents of Exorcism in the Early Christian Period: All Christians, Any Christians, or a Select Few Christians?," *Antiphon* 16, no. 3 (2012): 198–203.

request to God to free a person). In some cases, the saints freed people by a mere touch from themselves in life, or from their relics after their death. An example of this type comes from Jerome's *Life of St. Hilarion*, a non-ordained monk:

> Next, holding both the man's hands tight, he trod on both his feet, muttering at the same time, "Here is torture for you, you crowd of demons, here is torture for you." When Orion screamed as his head touched the ground, his neck bent back, Hilarion said, "O Lord Jesus, release this poor man, release this captive. As you have the power to overcome one, so you can overcome many." I shall now tell you something very strange: from the mouth of this one man different voices were heard, sounding like the confused babble of a crowd. In this way Orion was cured.[92]

This exorcism was performed through touch, and a request to Jesus to free the man. Some effect seems operative in the touch of the saint. In the exorcisms performed by Jesus, there is no mention of touch (though there is when Jesus healed physical maladies). This focus on the body of the saint was perhaps a reaction to the increased devotion to relics of saints in this time period. Regardless, we see a different kind of exorcism here, a kind of charismatic exorcism, where a gift of the Holy Spirit seems to be operative in the touch of the saint, followed by a prayer that caused Jesus to free the man.

There are four such stories of exorcisms performed by St. Hilarion in Jerome's book on him. In them, demons show many

[92] Jerome, *Life of Hilarion*, trans. Carolinne White, in *Early Christian Lives*, ed. Carolinne White (New York: Penguin, 1998), 17; Latin original: *Vita Hilarionis*, 10.5–10 (SC, vol. 508, p. 240).

signs of possession: extraordinary strength, levitation, knowledge of hidden things, and the ability to speak languages the person did not know. These signs would continue to be seen through time in disparate cases, leading to them being cited as proofs of possession in the later rites of exorcism.

Exorcisms performed by non-ordained holy men and women in this time were considered charismatic exorcisms. These were not average people with these charisms, but were usually very prayerful, devout, ascetic, chaste, and often graced with other mystical experiences and phenomena.[93]

Traditio Apostolica (375–400) provides some details of pre-baptismal exorcisms practiced in Rome.[94] Pre-baptismal exorcisms were daily, early in the morning, and were performed by priests, deacons, ordained exorcists, or lay exorcists. On the day of their Baptisms, catechumens (candidates for Baptism) would be exorcised by the bishop's *exsufflation*, or blowing on them. Finally, they were anointed by the Oil of Catechumens before their Baptism. This was an oil that had been blessed by the bishop for this purpose. The catechumens had to be nude at their Baptism, and only eat exorcised bread before, both indicative of being free from all outside demonic influence.[95] These pre-baptismal exorcisms were not done because the catechumens were presumed to be possessed, but to restore them to as spiritually pristine a condition as possible before Baptism.

[93] Van Slyke, "The Human Agents of Exorcism in the Early Christian Period," p. 207.

[94] P. F. Bradshaw, M. E. Johnson, and L. E. Phillips, *The Apostolic Tradition: A Commentary* (Minneapolis, MN: Fortress Press, 2002).

[95] A. Nicolotti, *Esorcismo Cristiano e Possessione Diabolica tra II e III Secolo* (Turnhout: Brepols, 2011), p. 681.

They were done to address the indirect presence of the devil in the form of Original Sin. The idea of Original Sin being in a person was not developed until Augustine of Hippo (AD 354–430) first used the phrase *Original Sin*.

After a debate between Augustine and Pelagius the idea of Original Sin was accepted,[96] and it changed the character of pre-baptismal exorcism. By the mid-fourth century, many Christians believed an evil spirit was actually exorcised from the catechumen before Baptism. Augustine seems to have a more nuanced view: he viewed pre-baptismal exorcism as "a dramatic metaphor for the redemption of souls from their diabolical oppressor."[97]

In the middle of the third century, in Rome, there were fifty-two exorcists, readers, and doorkeepers in addition to the priests, deacons, subdeacons, and acolytes. We do not know the proportion of that fifty-two that were exorcists, but the exorcists existed. We know from Pseudo-Ambrose that by the fourth century, exorcist was a minor order of the clergy, "For a priest and the deacons enact the office of both exorcist and reader."[98]

Pope Innocent I (AD 401–417) introduced a further restriction on exorcisms performed by clergy. In his letter to Decentius of Gubbio, he says that a priest or deacon may lay hands on a person possessed after Baptism only with express permission from his bishop.[99] "Express" means a clear and outward expression,

[96] Nicolotti, *Esorcism Cristiano*, p. 86; Kelly, *The Devil at Baptism*, pp. 112–115.

[97] Kelly, *The Devil at Baptism*, p. 113.

[98] Ambrosiaster, *Quaestiones Veteris et Novi Testamenti*, 101.4 (*PL*, vol. 35, p. 2302).

[99] R. Cabié, *La lettre du pape Innocent 1st à Décentius de Gubbio (19 mars 416)* (Louvain: Publications Universitaires de Louvain: 1973), 2.102–112, p. 28.

not presumed or implied approval. This change did at least two things. It clarified that the exorcist worked with the power of authority held by the Church and not their own charism, and it kept the activity of the exorcist in the bishop's control.

Pope Innocent I's action to restrict the activity of exorcists was followed up at the Council of Laodicea (sometime in the mid-fourth century).[100] Canon 26 of that council prohibits people from doing exorcisms unless they are appointed by the bishop.[101] This made it unlawful for laity to perform charismatic exorcisms. There were a number of other councils from AD 305 to 692 that *in part* sought to correct abuses in exorcisms. These included The Council of Elvira (AD 305), the First Council of Orange (AD 441), the Eleventh Council of Toledo (AD 657),[102] and the Synod of Constantinople (AD 692). There was also a development of the criteria to diagnose possession and a punishment for people faking possession.

In spite of these restrictions on exorcism and exorcists, the fifth and sixth centuries saw continued cases of demoniacs being liberated by touching the relics, or tombs, of saints, of charismatic exorcisms performed by lay men and women, as well as the approved function of clergy appointed to do exorcisms by their

[100] E. Landon, *A Manual of Councils of the Holy Catholic Church*, vol. 1 (Edinburgh, J. Grant: 1909), pp. 317–318.

[101] C. Hefele, *A History of the Councils of the Church: From the Original Documents*, trans. H. Oxenham, 5 vols. (Edinburgh: T and T Clark, 1986), vol. 2, p. 411; *Sacrorum Conciliorum Nova et Amplissima Collectio*, ed. J. Mansi, 31 vols. (Paris: H. Welter, 1901–1927), vol. 2, cols. 567–568.

[102] Hefele, *A History of the Councils of the Church*, vol. 1, pp. 148–152; vol. 3, p. 162; vol. 4, p. 489; *Sacrorum Conciliorum Nova et Amplissima Collectio*, vol. 2, cols. 10–12; vol. 6, cols. 438–439; vol. 11, col. 145.

bishops.[103] Pope St. Gregory the Great (AD 540–604) reported on a number of exorcisms in Italy performed by non-clergy in his time. Three examples were performed by St. Benedict. In the first case, he exorcised a cleric who was vexed by demons, this exorcism being done by praying to God.[104] In another case, he freed one of his monks by striking him with a rod.[105] In a third case, Benedict freed an old monk by slapping him.[106] Gregory emphasizes two points after reviewing a number of exorcisms: evil spirits are entirely subject to God, and God's servants find strength against evil spirits though humility and obedience.

The earliest reference to a Church-produced rite of exorcism appears in the *Gregorian Sacramentary* (AD 595). The rite it refers to has not survived. It formalized the clerical order of exorcist as a minor order. During the ordination of an exorcist, it says:

> When the exorcist is ordained, he receives from the hand of the bishop a small book in which are written the exorcisms. The bishop says to him: Receive and commit to memory, and have the power to lay hands upon energumens, either baptized or catechumen.[107]

This was a significant development. Previously, exorcists had usually been non-ordained laypeople who only worked with the possessed outside of pre-baptismal rites, and in undefined ways.

[103] Van Slyke, "The Human Agents of Exorcism in the Early Christian Period," pp. 214–215.

[104] Gregory the Great, *Dialogues*, 2.16.1 (*SC*, vol. 260, pp. 184–186).

[105] Gregory the Great, *Dialogues*, 2.4.2–3 (*SC*, vol. 260, pp. 152).

[106] Gregory the Great, *Dialogues*, 2.30.1 (*SC*, vol. 260, pp. 220).

[107] Hefele, *A History of the Councils of the Church*, vol. 2, p. 411; *Sacrorum Conciliorum Nova et Amplissima Collectio*, vol. 3, col. 951.

Now, the exorcist was ordained clergy who could only work in defined ways with both the possessed and the non-possessed catechumens in preparation for Baptism. It is important to note that there is no reported case of a married Christian performing an exorcism in the entire early history of the Church. This supports the position that not all baptized Christians are empowered to cast out demons. Those that did have this power were either clerics exercising the authority of the Church, or were holy single people that God endowed with a particular charism, the exercise of which was now unlawful to apply in exorcism.

From the late sixth century through the seventh century there is a steep decline in the written references to exorcists or exorcisms.[108] The functions that specifically ordained exorcists, who were clergy with minor clerical orders but not full priests, performed were taken over by clergy of higher orders (priests).[109] The work of exorcists in previous centuries did not have a fixed form; each practitioner improvised their own way of doing exorcisms. The book that exorcists received at ordination was a *libellus*, a *locally produced* pamphlet of prayers, texts, and rubrics (rules). There were no universal rites, missals, or sacramentaries in those centuries.[110]

Then we have the *Ordo Romanius XI* (AD 650), a collection of Roman rites written in the late sixth or seventh century. It

[108] J. Russell, *Lucifer: The Devil in the Middle Ages* (Ithaca, NY: Cornell University Press, 1984), p. 124.

[109] H. A. Kelly, *The Devil, Demonology, and Witchcraft: The Development of Christian Beliefs in Evil Spirits* (Garden City, NY: Doubleday, 1968), p. 83.

[110] C. Hanson, "The Liberty of the Bishop to Improvise Prayer in the Eucharist," in *Vigiliae Christianae* 15, no. 3 (September 1961): p. 174.

included a liturgy for pre-baptismal exorcism of infants, which included this rebuke to the devil by a first acolyte:

> Therefore, accursed devil, recognize your sentence and give honour to the living and true God, give honour to Jesus Christ his Son, draw back from this servant of God, because God himself and our Lord Jesus Christ deigns to call these [catechumens] to his holy grace and blessing, the font, and the gift of baptism; by this sign of the cross on their foreheads, which we give and which you, accursed devil, may never dare to violate.[111]

Then they were signed with the cross, and a second acolyte laid hands on them, saying:

> Hear, accursed Satan, adjured by the name of the eternal God and our Saviour, the Son of God, depart having been defeated, trembling and groaning, with your envy. Let there be nothing in common between you and the servants of God, now contemplating heavenly things, about to renounce you and your world, and about to win a blessed immortality. Therefore give honour to the coming Holy Spirit.[112]

Finally, a third acolyte also signed them with the Cross and laid hands on them, saying:

> I exorcise you, unclean spirit, so that in the name of the Father, of the Son, and of the Holy Spirit, you should go out and draw back from these servants of God. For

[111] *Ordo XI*, 14 (*OR*, vol. 2, p. 421).
[112] *Ordo XI*, 18 (*OR*, vol. 2, p. 422).

> he himself commands you, accursed [and] damned one, who opened the eyes of the man born blind and raised Lazarus from the tomb on the fourth day.[113]

We find one more exorcistic part of the *Ordo XI* rite of pre-baptismal exorcism on the morning of Holy Saturday:

> Nor does it escape you, Satan, that punishments threaten you, torments threaten you, the day of judgement threatens you, the day of punishment, the day that is to come like a burning furnace, in which eternal perdition will come for you and all your angels. Therefore, damned one, give honour to the living and true God, give honour to Jesus Christ his Son, and to the Holy Spirit, in whose name and power I command you to go out and depart from this servant of God, whom today the Lord our God Jesus Christ has deigned to call by his gift to his holy grace and to the blessing and font of baptism, that he may become his temple by the water of regeneration for the remission of all sins.[114]

In Northern Europe, Christianity was advancing into new lands and cultures, so the need for pre-baptismal exorcisms of adults increased there. At the beginning of the seventh century, the Church produced the Gelasian Sacramentary, compiled from various primitive sources, in Chelles, France.[115] It was a book that had everything a parish priest needed to function in that region of the world. There was a rite for "making a catechumen

[113] *Ordo XI*, 21–22 (*OR*, vol. 2, p. 423).

[114] *Ordo XI*, 83–84.

[115] C. Vogel, *Medieval Liturgy: An Introduction to the Sources*, trans. W. Storey and N. Rasmussen (Pastoral Press, 1981), p. 64–65.

from a pagan." The adult pagan was instructed to be in horror of the pagan idols. The anointing was understood to protect the catechumen from the devil re-entering them at a later time. This indicated a clearer understanding that the devil was being driven out before the Baptism.[116]

There was a supplement of the Gelasian Sacramentary that dealt with demonic oppression and possession in energumens (not catechumens preparing for Baptism), and how to exorcise them.[117] The Gregorian Sacramentary was produced in Rome later in the seventh century. It included many of the same exorcism prayers as the Gelasian Sacramentary, but they were no longer relegated to a supplement.[118]

The Gellone Sacramentary (AD 790), which was primarily a history of the Roman liturgy, has an exorcism rite for an adult energumen, and also one for infants who are not baptized.[119] The rite for an adult energumen culminates in three "great adjurations":[120]

1. I adjure you, therefore ancient serpent. *Adiuro ergo te serpens antique.*
2. I adjure you, not by my weakness but in the power of the Holy Spirit. *Adiuro te, non mea infirmitate sed in virtute spiritus sancti.*

[116] Alcuin, *Epistula*, 134, 137, in *Epistulae Karolini Aevi*, vol. 2, ed. E. Dümmler, Monumenta Germaniae Historia 4 (Berlin: Weidmann, 1895), pp. 202–203, 210–216.

[117] E. A. Lowe, "The Vatican MS of the Gelasian Sacramentary and Its Supplement at Paris," *Journal for Theological Studies* 27, no. 108 (July 1926): pp. 357–373, at p. 360.

[118] *The Gregorian Sacramentary under Charles the Great*, ed. H. Wilson, Henry Bradshaw Society (London: Harrison, 1915).

[119] *Sacramentarium Gellonensis*, 2401.

[120] *Sacramentarium Gellonensis*, 2405.

3. I adjure you, therefore, most wicked dragon. *Adiuro ergo te, draco quiessime.*

Some of the Gellone Sacramentary rite of exorcism is similar to the pre-baptismal rite of exorcism found in *Ordo XI* (AD 650), but it mainly avoided that language of the pre-baptismal exorcism. Seven sections of the Gellone Sacramentary rite appear later in the AD 1614 rite of exorcism.[121]

Another exorcism rite for energumens, from the Gelasian Sacramentary (AD 750), has ten adjurations and borrows much language from the *Ordo XI* pre-baptismal exorcism rite.[122] Five sections of the Gelasian Sacramentary rite of exorcism appear in the AD 1614 rite of exorcism.[123] The Gelasian Sacramentary also had a pre-baptismal exorcism rite (for adults and infants), special exorcisms for sick catechumens and possessed catechumens, and a post-baptismal exorcism using the Oil of Chrism.[124]

Exorcism in the Middle Ages, 900–1517

Exorcism early in this period became less well regulated, both in what rites were used and what they were used for. In some parts of Europe, exorcism was used for medical problems, temptations, mental illness, and possession.[125] There also was poor criteria

[121] Young, *A History of Exorcism in Catholic Christianity*, p. 49.

[122] Paris, Bibliotheque Nationale, MS Lat. 7193, fols. 41–56; edited text in Lowe, "The Vatican MS of the Gelasian Sacramentary and Its Supplement at Paris," pp. 360–365.

[123] Young, *A History of Exorcism in Catholic Christianity*, p. 51.

[124] *Sacramentarium Gellonensis*, 2344–2386, 384.

[125] F. Chave-Mahir, *L'Exorcisme des Possédés dans l'Eglise d'Occident (Xe–XIVe siècle)* (Turnhout: Brepols, 2011), p. 23; M. Sluhovsky, *Believe Not Every Spirit: Possession, Mysticism and Discernment in*

for discerning between these. Symptoms of possession included shouting, swearing, dumbness, paralysis, and body contortions. Varying ancient formulas were often used as there was less organization and regulation by the Church. Theologians continued to be interested in the topics of demonology, possession, and exorcism, but they were not practicing exorcists.[126]

Peter Lombard (AD 1100–1160) discussed exorcism in his main work, *Sentences*.[127] In his treatment of catechizing and exorcising the neophyte, he makes the first distinction between a sacrament and a sacramental, but he does not definitively resolve which an exorcism is.[128] Later, the exorcism rite would be categorized as a sacramental. A sacrament is an action of the Church where the action of God is guaranteed. A sacramental does not have a guaranteed action, but relies on the prayer of the Church and what response God chooses to give.

Thomas Aquinas (AD 1225–1274) sought to clarify and defend the Catholic Faith at a time of debate and struggle with heretical breakaway groups. As part of his work, he wrote a large amount on angels, so much so that he is referred to as the "Angelic Doctor." He provides material relevant to understanding possession and exorcism: the nature of angels, the fall of the evil angels, why the devil opposes God, how the

---

Early Modern Catholicism (Chicago, IL: University of Chicago Press, 2007), p. 14.

[126] Young, *A History of Exorcism in Catholic Christianity*, p.61.

[127] "Peter Lombard," in *The Oxford Dictionary of the Christian Church*, p. 1275.

[128] L. Eisenhofer and J. Lechner, *The Liturgy of the Roman Rite*, ed. H. Winstone, trans. A. Peeler and E. Peeler (New York: Herder and Herder, 1961), p. 337; also J. Huels, "A Juridical Notion of Sacramentals," *StC* 38 (2004): p. 346.

demons interact with people, and how they possess them. He also gives some specific opinions about exorcism. He says it is permissible to adjure demons to depart a person, but one is to avoid seeking hidden knowledge or any other favor from the demon.[129] A baptized person who is oppressed or possessed is not to be refused Communion.[130] A pre-baptismal exorcism is a sacramental that prepares the catechumen for the Sacrament of Baptism.[131] Finally, the work of the exorcist should be done by the minor order exorcist, not the priest.[132]

Thomas addresses the question "Whether it is lawful to adjure the demons?" in his *Summa Theologica*. He first defines *adjure* as to "induce anyone to do a certain thing for the sake of God's name." Based on Mark 16:17, "In my name they will drive out demons," it is lawful to adjure demons to repulse them so that they do not harm soul or body. It is not lawful to adjure them to learn something from them, or obtain some favor from them.[133] This is the critical difference between religion and magic

[129] Thomas Aquinas, *Summa Theologica* II–II, q. 90, art. 2, in *Summa Theologiae*, vol. 39, trans. K. O'Rourke, Blackfriars (London: Eyre and Spottiswoode, 1964), pp. 238–241.

[130] Aquinas, *Summa Theologica* III, q. 80, art. 9, in *Summa Theologiae*, vol. 59, trans. T. Gilby, Blackfriars (London: Eyre and Spottiswoode, 1975), pp. 70–73.

[131] Aquinas, *Summa Theologica* III, q. 71, art. 2–3, in *Summa Theologiae*, vol. 57, trans. J. Cunningham, Blackfriars, (London: Eyre and Spottiswoode, 1975), pp. 174–181; see also Aquinas, *Summa Theologica* III, q. 65, a. 1.

[132] Aquinas, *Summa Theologica* III, q. 71, art. 4, in *Summa Theologiae*, vol. 57, pp. 182–185.

[133] Aquinas, *Summa Theologica* II–II, q. 90, art. 2, in *Summa Theologica*, trans. Fathers of the English Dominican Province (New York: Benziger, 1947; online ed. CCEL), https://www.ccel.org/ccel/aquinas/summa.SS_Q90_A2.html.

for Thomas. His reasoning is that demons are our enemies, and to hold friendship with them is therefore unlawful. In a related way, he says that adjuration to any end (even repulsing them) sought through friendly appeal to the demons is unlawful. Thomas was addressing the blurring between exorcism and magical practices that crept in during his time. He also was generally condemning magic as being unlawful.

From the eleventh to the thirteenth centuries, there was an increase in exorcisms and an increase in abuses. Some exorcists started administering medicines to the energumens, as well as using other paraphernalia based on superstitions.[134] There were also strange outbreaks of apparent group possessions that occurred, particularly in convents. Exorcism in some places was treated as a spectacle for the people. A disordered perspective took hold that demons were behind everything bad in the world. The Church tried to reign in these abuses by limiting who could be an exorcist, and what methods they could employ, but this did not affect public opinion much.[135]

In the 1200s, exorcism continued to be associated with particular saints, both living and dead. This emphasis on the saints increased, and exorcism rites all but disappeared from liturgical books. Then the Cathar heresy, a Gnostic heresy that proposed

[134] A. Goddu, "The Failure of Exorcism in the Middle Ages," in *Possession and Exorcism*, ed. B. Levack, Articles on Witchcraft, Magic and Demonology, vol. 9 (New York: Garland, 1992), p. 11.

[135] A. Franz, *Die Kirchlichen Benediktionen im Mittelalter*, vol. 2 (Graz: Akademische Druck und Verlagsanstalt, 1960), pp. 567-572, 642-643. This reprint of the original 1909 work deals primarily with exorcistic formulas while offering extensive insight into medieval demonology.

a good god of the New Testament and an evil god of the Old Testament, forced the Church to reexamine the theology of evil, which naturally led to a reexamination of demonology, possession, and exorcism. In AD 1215, the Fourth Lateran Council produced a dogmatic definition of demons:[136]

> The devil and other demons were created by God naturally good, but they became evil by their own doing.[137]

The Dominican order was founded in 1216, largely in response to the heresies and debates that had arisen at that time. Its main charism was teaching the Faith and refuting error. It produced many philosophers and theologians, and was a largely intellectual order. It also sought to address witchcraft, which became a serious concern in the Middle Ages. Most of the inquisitors, which were judges of non-Catholic Christians, in the next few centuries were chosen from the Dominican order.

By the 1300s, exorcism was being rediscovered, but aspects of ritual magic were being incorporated into the ancient rites of the Church. At the same time, there was a decline in the number of exorcisms associated with saints, creating a perceived crisis in exorcism.[138] Then in 1378, the Papal Schism happened, and the authority of the Church was challenged. Exorcism was appropriated back from the realm of the saints and used as a sign of

[136] On Lateran IV's definition of *demons*, see P. Quay, "Angels and Demons: The Teaching of IV Lateran," *Theological Studies* 42, no. 1 (1981), pp. 20–45.

[137] Lateran Council IV, Confession of Faith (November 30, 1215), https://www.papalencyclicals.net/councils/ecum12-2.htm

[138] A. Goddu, *Soziale Ordnungen im Selbstverständnis des Mittelalters*, Miscellanea Mediaevalia 12/2 (Berlin: Walter de Gruyter, 1980), pp. 552–557.

legitimate Church authority.[139] Exorcism was increasingly framed as a war between angels and demons, and it became associated with apocalyptic ideas.[140]

An exorcism book from about 1400 contains examples of the integration of nonsense magical incantations into exorcism. In it the priest is instructed:

> Take the head of the possessed in your left hand and place your thumb in the mouth of the possessed, saying the following words to both ears: "Rise up again from here *abrya*, rise up again from here, things consecrated together *ypar ytumba opote alacent alaphie*."[141]

This exorcism also used Greek and Hebrew names for God: *Agla*, *Tetragrammaton*, *Ysiton*, and *Pneumator*, a feature that was common in magical rituals of the time.[142]

Another practice that blurred the line between magic and exorcism was the use of paper amulets, usually with Scripture written on them.[143] In a book on the life of St. Anthony of Padua from 1367, a woman tempted to suicide was visited by St. Anthony in a dream. In the dream he gave her a parchment amulet with these words:

139 Caciola, *Discerning Spirits*, pp. 236–237.

140 Caciola, *Discerning Spirits*, pp. 264–267.

141 Munich, Bayerische Staatsbibliothek, MS Clm 10085, fol. 3V, quoted in Chave-Mahir, *L'Exorcisme des Possédés dans l'Eglise d'Occident*, p. 325.

142 Chave-Mahir, *L'Exorcisme des Possédés dans l'Eglise d'Occident*, pp. 325–326.

143 D. C. Skemer, *Binding Words: Textual Amulets in the Middle Ages* (University Park, PA: Pennsylvania State University Press, 2006), pp. 47–49, 175.

> Behold the cross of Christ! Flee, hostile powers! The lion from the tribe of Judah and the root of David vanquishes! Alleluia! Alleluia![144]

These words were included in the 1614 rite of exorcism, as well as appearing on the obelisk outside of St. Peter's basilica in Rome as:

> Behold the Cross of the Lord! Be gone, all evil powers! The Lion of the tribe of Judah, The root of David has conquered! Alleluia!

We see a modern example of these exorcistic amulets today: the popular St. Benedict Medal. On the reverse side are the first letters of a Latin adjuration against the devil:

> Begone, Satan! Never tempt me with your vanities! What you offer me is evil. Drink the poison yourself![145]

The printing press was invented around 1436 in Germany. It led to the number of different exorcism rites increasing rapidly. These small, portable books usually combined ancient exorcism rites with litanies of the saints, prayers against witchcraft, and even pharmaceutical recipes.[146] This began a new era of exorcism, where the exorcist with his book took on the prominence the

[144] Young, F. A History of Exorcism in Catholic Christianity. Palgrave Mcmillian, Switzerland, 2016, p. 75.

[145] D. Lederer, *Madness, Religion and the State in Early Modern Europe: A Bavarian Beacon* (Cambridge, MA: Cambridge University Press, 2005), pp. 226, 232. Also see "The Medal of Saint Benedict," osb.org, accessed March 13, 2023, https://www.osb.org/gen/medal.html.

[146] Caciola, *Discerning Spirits*, pp. 239–241.

saints and their tombs had had before.[147] We see the development of structured questioning of the demon during this time. The demon was now asked its name, and to which level of demons it belonged.[148] There was also an increased emphasis on the diagnostic criteria for possession, and proving objectively that a person was possessed.[149] One diagnostic test was secretly placing a pyx with a consecrated host on the person's head. If the demon were able to identify what was in the pyx, that was supportive of the possession hypothesis in that case.

This is not to say there had never been examples of demonic interrogation before. Exorcism rites varied greatly, and different techniques were used in different places. Bede (673–735) wrote on the exorcists' questioning of demons in England:

> And they command the name of the demon, which they would say to be forbidden, and the means of swearing oaths by which each pledged a pact of love to the other should be produced.[150]

This shows an early importance to the name of the demon, and by what right it had possession of the person, presuming that right was some agreement the person made with it.

A curious development specific to English culture and exorcism in the Middle Ages is that they were more worried about possessed corpses than living people. English folklore commonly included *revenants*, or animated bodies, or zombies. One friar's

[147] Chave-Mahir, *L'Exorcisme des Possédés dans l'Eglise d'Occident*, p. 330.

[148] Caciola, *Discerning Spirits*, pp. 244–248.

[149] Young, *A History of Exorcism in Catholic Christianity*, p. 77.

[150] Bede, *In Lucae Evangelium Expositio* (*PL*, vol, 92, p. 438B).

solution to one such revenant was to decapitate the animated body.[151] Also common in England was the idea of ghosts, which the Sign of the Cross or saints' relics would drive off. The word *coniuro* was also used against ghosts, and they were even sometimes interrogated in a similar way to demons.[152]

From the fourteenth through the seventeenth centuries, the paranoia about witchcraft worsened in the Western world. A systematic search for witches in communities, as well as their trials and punishments, was instituted.[153] These witch hunts became enmeshed with exorcism ministry in an unhealthy way. Many people did not understand the difference between witches and the possessed. Exorcism was used on purported witches against their will, and without a desire to liberate them from a demon. When exorcism was seen to be ineffective in "curing" the witches, it became devalued in the eyes of many in the Church.

A Dominican theologian, Johannes Nider (1380–1438) wrote *Formicarius* in 1438, in which he tried to distinguish the possessed from witches, as well as from the mentally ill.[154] After presenting a number of cases that he witnessed himself, he concluded that

[151] S. M. Butler, "Cultures of Suicide? Suicide Verdicts and the 'Community' in Thirteenth- and Fourteenth-Century England," *Historian* 69, no. 3 (2007): pp. 427–449, at p. 436.

[152] J. Simpson, "Repentant Soul or Walking Corpse: Debatable Apparitions in Medieval England," *Folklore* 114, no. 3 (2003): pp. 389–402.

[153] For an exhaustive study of the development of witchcraft and its repercussions in early modern Europe, see S. Clark, *Thinking with Demons: The Idea of Wtchcraft in Early Modern Europe* (Oxford: Clarendon Press, 1997); see also J. Russell, *Witchcraft in the Middle Ages* (Ithaca, NY: Cornell University, 1972).

[154] See J. Nyder, *Formicarius*, ed. H. Biedermann (Graz: Akademische Druck und Verlagsanstalt, 1971).

"such people often have more need for a physician to cure their body than one for their soul."[155]

In 1484, two Dominican inquisitors, or witch hunters, Heinrich Kramer and Jacob Sprenger, were barred from working in Germany due to their abuses. They appealed to Pope Innocent VIII for help. This led to the papal bull *Summis desiderantes affectibus*, which was promulgated on December 5, 1484. A quote from *Summis desiderantes affectibus* conveys the prevailing view of witches and witchcraft at the time:

> Many persons of both sexes, unmindful of their own salvation and straying from the Catholic Faith, have abandoned themselves to devils, incubi and succubi, and by their incantations, spells, conjurations, and other accursed charms and crafts, enormities and horrid offences, have slain infants yet in the mother's womb, as also the offspring of cattle, have blasted the produce of the earth, the grapes of the vine, the fruits of the trees, nay, men and women, beasts of burden, herd-beasts, as well as animals of other kinds, vineyards, orchards, meadows, pasture-land, corn, wheat, and all other cereals; these wretches furthermore afflict and torment men and women, beasts of burden, herd-beasts, as well as animals of other kinds, with terrible and piteous pains and sore diseases, both internal and external; they hinder men from performing the sexual act and women from conceiving ... they blasphemously renounce that Faith which is theirs by the Sacrament of Baptism, and at the instigation of the Enemy of Mankind they do not shrink

[155] Rodewyk, *Possessed by Satan*, p. 44.

> from committing and perpetrating the foulest abominations and filthiest excesses to the deadly peril of their own souls ... the abominations and enormities in question remain unpunished not without open danger to the souls of many and peril of eternal damnation.[156]

Emboldened by this papal action, Kramer and Sprenger published their guidebook for inquisitors, the *Malleus Maleficarum* (*The Hammer of Witches*) in 1486. The book reproduced the papal bull, which lent it great credibility and popularity. It was not the only book on this topic, but it became by far the best known. Because the book encouraged the mistreatment of alleged witches, *the Church condemned the book as unethical and illegal, and then banned it.*[157] Regardless, the book remained in circulation and had two effects relevant to this topic. First, it stated that exorcism is useless against witches and their magic, and so exorcism was banned in some regions. Second, it sparked the European witch trials, which killed as many as eighty thousand people from 1500 to 1600.

During this nadir in the history of exorcism, the Church tried to bring order back by starting to provide specific criteria to substantiate possession, as well as guidelines for exorcists. Not much progress was made. Henry of Gorkum (d. 1413), another Dominican, prepared some basic instructions on performing exorcisms.[158]

In the sixteenth century, exorcism was largely seen as an archaic practice that had largely failed through the Middle Ages.

[156] Innocent VIII, Bull *Summis desiderantes affectibus* (December 5, 1484).

[157] Goddu, "The Failure of Exorcism in the Middle Ages," p. 15.

[158] Rodewyk, *Possessed by Satan*, p. 48.

An effort was started to save the ministry. Girolamo Menghi (1529–1609), a Franciscan, studied medieval manuscripts and gathered much data on demonology and exorcism. This, combined with his success as an exorcist, led him to being called the "father of the exorcist's art."[159] Menghi wrote a number of books on exorcism, and critically included practical tips for the exorcist on how to discern spirits and perform exorcisms well.[160] A concise list of these tips was generated by the translator Gaetano Paxia, and is reproduced here:

1. Exorcists must have great faith in their mission; they must be moved by a desire to glorify God. It is God who is operating here.
2. Exorcists must prepare for the prayers of exorcism by fasting and abstinence, which refine the spirit and keep concupiscence at bay.
3. Exorcisms must be celebrated following the rites and customs of the Catholic Church. Menghi incessantly exalts the role of the community in the rites.
4. Before taking up the concrete action of exorcism, ministers must be sure they are facing a case of true diabolic possession, not one requiring the intervention of doctors, astrologers, or theologians.
5. Exorcists must constantly illustrate and clarify the exorcistic activity: a purely spiritual work, highly worthy in the eyes of God. In no way must there be cause for scandal or evil (*ruina*) toward those present.[161]

[159] G. Menghi, *The Devil's Scourge: Exorcism during the Italian Renaissance*, ed. and trans. G. Paxia (York Beach, ME: Weiser Books, 2002), p. 16.

[160] Menghi, *The Devil's Scourge*, pp. 31–32.

[161] Menghi, *The Devil's Scourge*, pp. 34.

In addition to these, he suggests that exorcisms be performed in sacred places, that exorcists never be left alone with the energumen, that exorcists not question the demon out of curiosity, and that there not be too many in attendance.[162]

Peter Thyraecus (1546–1601), a Jesuit, produced a list of the signs of genuine possession. These were:

1. Knowledge of hidden things.
2. Knowledge of languages the person has never learned.
3. Abnormal strength.
4. Great suffering from contact with sacred things.[163]

The common feature of Thyraecus' signs of possession is that they defy natural explanations.

The *Roman Ritual* of 1614

Pope Paul V (1605–1621) appointed a commission to create the *Roman Ritual* book for the Church in 1612. This was inspired by the Council of Trent. This would include all of the rituals a parish priest would need in the running of a parish, including exorcism of an energumen. A year later, it was completed, and he introduced it with the papal bull *Apostolicae sedi* on June 17, 1614.[164] This new ritual did not abrogate (remove) the local rituals in use around the world, and the use of this new ritual

[162] Menghi, *The Devil's Scourge*, pp. 33, 36–37.

[163] P. Thyraeus, *Daemoniaci, Hoc Est: De Obsessis a Spiritibus Daemoniorum Hominibus* (Cologne: Agrippina, 1598), p. 98.

[164] *Rituale Romanum: Pauli V Pontificis Maximi jussu editum* (1614; Rome: Typis Polyglottis Vaticanis, 1957). Extant copies of the original *Roman Ritual* of 1614 are rare. Fortunately, the Monumenta Liturgica Concilii Tridentini series has reproduced an analytical edition with introduction and appendices. See *Rituale*

was only suggested. Nevertheless, it was disseminated rapidly and gave, for the first time, a universal and standard ritual of the Roman Catholic Church. It would remain in use for three and a half centuries.

The Exorcism Rite of 1614

Many sources, much thought, and extensive experience went into creating the exorcism rite in the *Roman Ritual* of 1614. The primary source was *Rituale Sacramentorum Romanum Gregorii XIII*, written by Santori in 1584. Santori's predecessors, Castellani and Samarino, were also used. Santori used the work of Menghi and Thyraecus in the *praenotanda*. In addition, there were many local rites of exorcism in use that were consulted. St. Charles Borromeo (1538–1584), through a number of councils he presided over and worked on, contributed greatly to the guidelines that introduced the rite. These guidelines were produced under St. Borromeo, but not all were ultimately printed in the rite. The instructions from the rite are summarized here, with notation in brackets as needed:

1. A priest must have express [clear, outward, usually written] and special [case-by-case] permission [provides liceity] by the ordinary [allows for other superiors than the diocesan bishop to give permission] and be distinguished for piety, prudence, morals, and integrity of life. He should be older. He should be completely humble. He should only rely on divine power.

Romanum: Editio Princeps (1614), ed. M. Sodi and J. Arcas (Vatican City: Libreria Editrice Vaticana, 2004).

Item 1 originally said, "A priest, or any other legitimate minister of the Church," which allowed for clerics only ordained to the lower order of exorcists to perform exorcisms of people. This was changed since the promulgation of the 1917 Code of Canon Law.[165] The other change was in the first line of the rite, which then said, "A priest, or other exorcist"[166] and now says, "A priest delegated by the Ordinary."[167]

2. He should study the topic of exorcism by reading approved authors. He should learn from his own cases.
3. He should not easily believe a person is possessed. Signs of possession are: facility with languages the person does not know, revealing future or hidden things, abnormal strength, as well as "other indicators" that may be apparent.
4. Ask the energumen what they experienced during the exorcism. Ask what was most effective against the demon.
5. Be on guard against deception: deceptive answers, mumbling, tiring the exorcist out so he gives up, and pretending to leave the person.
6. If the person seems free, you should continue praying until you see the signs of deliverance [which are not described].

[165] "Sacerdos, seu quis alius legitimus Ecclesiae minister, vexatos a daemone exorcizaturus"; *Rituale Romanum:Editio Princeps (1614)*, p. 198.

[166] "Sacerdos, sive alius Exorcista"; Rituale *Romanum: Editio Princeps (1614)*, p. 200.

[167] "Sacerdos ab Ordinario delegatus"; *Roman Ritual: In Latin and English with Rubrics and Plainchant Notation*, vol. 2, pp. 174–175.

7. The demon will try to make the person not come to the exorcism, or convince them it is mental illness. They may make them fall asleep, or create an illusion in their perception. They may pretend to not be present.
8. The energumen should not go to sorcerers or necromancers [psychics and false healers].
9. Sometimes they pretend to leave, and the person can even receive Communion.
10. The exorcist should pray and fast. He should also encourage his team to do so.
11. The exorcism should take place in a church, or a holy place, away from crowds. If the person is ill, it can be done in his home.
12. The energumen should also pray, fast, receive the sacraments, and trust in God.
13. The exorcist should have a crucifix, and relics of the saints if available. The relics can be applied to the energumen's head. The Eucharist is not to be used during exorcisms.
14. Do not ask superfluous questions. Do not believe them if they pretend to be a dead person, a saint, or a holy angel.
15. Necessary questions are: the number and names of the demons in the person, when they entered, and how they entered. Ignore the bad behavior of the demon. The bystanders are not to talk to the demon.
16. Speak in a commanding and authoritative voice, with confidence, humility, and fervor. When the demon is in distress, pray harder. If the body becomes swollen or painful, trace the Sign of the Cross and apply holy water.

17. Repeat the words, or sections of the exorcism, that cause the demon the most distress. Pray for two to four hours, or more, if progress is being made.
18. Do not give, or recommend, any medicine to the energumen.
19. When praying with a woman, have female witnesses who will hold the woman. Do not allow anything inappropriate to happen.
20. Do not use prayers you have created, but use Holy Scripture. Make the demon reveal if the person has consumed a cursed object, or has one hidden on his person. If so, try to get them and destroy them. The energumen should reveal their temptations to the exorcist.
21. After they are freed, they have to be careful and not fall back into sin, lest the demon be able to return.

The rite of exorcism starts with the Litany of the Saints. This is common of many rites of the Church in the *Roman Ritual* of 1614. It is also likely inspired by the time in the Church's history when the saints were called upon to do exorcisms. It includes eleven psalms, calling back to the Jewish tradition of David's exorcising king Saul with a song, four Gospel readings, which remind the priest and the demon of the victory of Christ over them, and the Athanasian Creed, which is a powerful statement of faith. There are also four lengthy exorcistic prayers with strong, and poetic commands to depart the energumen. In addition, the exorcist is encouraged to pray standard traditional prayers, use holy water on the energumen, apply his stole, and make the Sign of the Cross. The currently available printing of the rite of exorcism from 1614 is twenty-five pages long.

There were two continuing issues with the ministry of exorcism over the next 251 years: Exorcists sometimes neglected to seek the bishop's permission to use the rite, and the embellishment of the rite by exorcists. Five Provincial Synods, Naples (AD 1699), Vienna (AD 1858), Venice (AD 1859), Prague (AD 1860), and Utrecht (AD 1865) make mention of problems with exorcisms.[168]

Exorcism in the Eighteenth and Nineteenth Centuries

Most Church authorities discouraged exorcism in the eighteenth and nineteenth centuries, as relations with secular governments were seen as very important.

At the end of the nineteenth century, Pope Leo XIII wrote the St. Michael exorcism after some sort of unusual experience he had. It was primarily directed at the Freemasons, which the popes had been speaking on since Freemasonry's inception in the early 1700s. It is worth reviewing the history of Freemasonry and the Church's position on it so that Pope Leo XIII's exorcism prayer of 1890 can be understood in proper historical context.

Freemasonry and the Church

Freemasonry is a global secret society comprised primarily of businessmen, male politicians, and other socially influential men. Freemasonry is sexist in that only men can join, and it is racist in that black men may not join. There is a form of Freemasonry for black men, often unrecognized by white Freemasons, called

[168] *Acta et Decreta Sacrorum Conciliorum Recentiorum: Collectio Lacensis*, 7 vols (Friburgi Brisgoviae: Herder, 1870–1882), vols. 1, 5, and 6.

Prince Hall Freemasonry. The position of the Catholic Church on Freemasonry, and particularly on membership in Freemasonry, is not clear to some of the public. This lack of clarity occurred because at the time it was not clear what the Church's position on membership in Freemasonry was.

In the Middle Ages (400–1500), there were many trade guilds in Europe. These were groups of workers in various trades such as carpentry, shipping, arts, and stone masonry. The guilds existed to ensure a minimum level of competency in work to the public, royalty, Church, and other institutions. Guilds also existed to regulate and protect trade secrets, and they included secret signs of membership to other guild members. A similar system is still in use today in many trades. For instance, there are apprentice electricians, journeyman electricians, licensed industrial electricians, and professional electrical engineers. There are also systems of licensing in many intellectual disciplines that involve apprenticeship, membership in a professional organization, and the oversight of the government through exams and other licensing requirements.

Most trade guilds in the Middle Ages were made up of indentured servants of the local royalty or Church: local workers who must work for their leaders. The Freemasons were stonemasons who were not bound to a local leader but were free to move about Europe as jobs required, hence "Free." They were initially a practical trade organization that did the stonework for many projects such as forts, castles, government buildings, and cathedrals through the Middle Ages. This type of Freemason, who did actual stonework, is called an "Operative Freemason" within Freemasonry today.

Operative Freemasons were generally of the religion of the region in which they worked, which was Catholic or Protestant in most cases. There are indications in early Operative Freemason documents that the organization was essentially Christian at that time. It is not clear how far back the Operative Freemason's guild goes. There are myths about the origins of Freemasonry going back to the building of Solomon's temple in the Old Testament, but these myths are not accepted by modern Freemason scholars.

Over time, other useful types of people were admitted to the Freemasonry organization: merchants, bankers, philosophers, and others. These were called "Accepted Masons" to delineate them from the Operative Freemasons. Over time this group of "Free and Accepted Masons" become less operative and more "speculative." This meant that they were less and less actual stonemasons and more of a social group.

On June 24, 1717, the Grand Lodge of England was formed and modern Freemasonry began. This "Modern Grand Lodge" was completely speculative, and it developed the blueprint for today's Masonic rituals. This blueprint included the three degrees of Freemasonry: entered apprentice, fellowcraft, and master mason. This group retained many traditions and symbols that were used in the Middle Ages by the Operative Freemasons, such as the square and compass that are used to lay out stones. This group quickly aligned with royalty and other people of influence by recruiting them to become members. It also tended to elect royal members as leaders of the group, which greatly accelerated its growth and influence.

By the early 1730s, in England, there were "Scotch masons" and "Scotch master masons." These were degrees beyond the master mason degree in the regular lodge. In 1745, the Grand Lodge of France gave the Scotch masons special privileges. By 1766, an elaborate sequence of degrees within the Scottish Rite were being developed in France. In its modern form, Scottish Rite Freemasonry has thirty-two degrees and one honorary degree.

Other variants of degree systems competed within various Freemasonry lodges in different countries, but the Scottish Rite thrived.

Some argue that modern Freemasonry is a system of thinking and government that emerged from the Protestant Reformation. Freemasonry emerged in a time when Enlightenment philosophy was a powerful force in European society. Church dogma and ecclesiastical authority were seen as oppressive by many, and the rational study of nature was championed. Freemasonry's degrees eliminated Christian prayer. They did, however, require a belief in a deity, the "Grand Architect of the Universe," and an afterlife. *The Constitution of the Free-Masons* (AD 1723), by Dr. James Anderson, states:

> Though in ancient Times Masons were charg'd in every Country to be of the Religion of that Country or Nation, whatever it was, yet 'tis now thought more expedient only to oblige them to that Religion in which all Men agree, leaving their particular Opinions to themselves.[169]

There was also a trend of rejecting royal authority in many countries, which would take a dramatic form later in the century during the American Revolution (1765–1783) and the French Revolution (1789–1799). Nine signers of the Declaration of Independence were Masons (16 percent), thirteen signers of the U.S. Constitution were Masons (33 percent), and fourteen U.S. presidents have been Freemasons. Notably, Benjamin Franklin, George Washington, and Andrew Jackson were Freemasons.

In modern North American Freemasonry, a thirty-second-degree Scottish Rite Mason, or a York Rite Mason in good

[169] J. Anderson, *The Constitutions of the Free-Masons*, 1734 (repr., London: Forgotten Books, 2019), "The Charges of a Free-Mason," 1.

standing, can join the Shriners. The Shriners are the "Ancient Arabic Order of the Nobles of the Mystic Shrine." They swear an oath to Allah on the Quran, promising under gruesome penalties to not disclose the secrets of their order. Shriners are most known for red fezzes (hats which are red in symbolism of the blood of Christians), parades, and children's hospitals.

There are auxiliary groups: the Order of the Eastern Star for women, DeMolay for boys, and Job's Daughters for girls. Other Masonic groups include Tall Cedars of Lebanon, the Mystic Order of Veiled Prophets of the Enchanted Realm, the Knights of Pythias, the Knights of the Red Cross of Constantine, the Independent Order of Odd Fellows, the Acacia Fraternity, the White Shrine of Jerusalem, the Order of the Rainbow, the Daughters of the Nile, the Order of Amaranth, and others.

There is no one central authority in Freemasonry; each Grand Lodge speaks for its state or region. There are *landmarks*, which are beliefs adopted by most Grand Lodges that give some uniformity to the beliefs and practices of Freemasonry. These include things like the belief in the Great Architect of the Universe, the belief in the soul, and the belief in the resurrection of the body.

Albert Pike (1809–1891) was the sovereign grand commander of the Southern Jurisdiction of the United States from 1859–1891. He is considered the father of Scottish Rite Freemasonry and he is a famous figure in the South in general. He is most remembered within Freemasonry for his book *Morals and Dogma of the Ancient and Accepted Scottish Rite of Freemasonry*. Here are some oft-cited quotes from this book:

> Lucifer, the Light-Bearer! Strange and mysterious name to give to the Spirit of Darkness! Lucifer, the Son of the Morning! Is it he who bears the light, and with its

splendors intolerable blinds feeble, sensual or selfish Souls? Doubt it not![170]

The devil is the personification of Atheism or Idolatry. For the Initiates, this is not a Person, but a Force, created for good, but which may serve for evil. It is the instrument of Liberty or Free Will. They represent this Force, which presides over the physical generation, under the mythological and horned form of the God Pan; thence came the he-goat of the Sabbat, brother of the Ancient Serpent, and the Light-bearer or Phosphor, of which the poets have made the false Lucifer of the legend.[171]

The true name of Satan, the Kabalists say, is Yahweh (GOD) reversed; for Satan is not a black god, but a negation of God ... the Kabala imagined Him to be a "most occult light."[172]

A perhaps more telling, but debated, quote is from *Albert Pike's Instructions to the 23 Supreme Councils of the World* (July 14, 1889):

That which we must say to a crowd is—We worship a God, but it is the God that one adores without superstition. To you, Sovereign Grand Inspectors General, we say this, that you may repeat it to the Brethren of the 32nd, 31st, and 30th degrees—The Masonic Religion should be, by all of us initiates of the high degrees, maintained

[170] A. Pike, *Morals and Dogma of the Ancient and Accepted Scottish Rite of Freemasonry*, 1872 (Washington DC: Supreme Council of the Thirty-Third Degree, 1964), p. 321.

[171] Pike, *Morals and Dogma*, p. 102.

[172] Pike, *Morals and Dogma*, p. 102.

> in the purity of the Luciferian Doctrine. If Lucifer were not God, would Adonay whose deeds prove his cruelty, perfidy and hatred of man, barbarism and repulsion for science, would Adonay and his priests, calumniate him? Yes, Lucifer is God, and unfortunately Adonay is also god. For the eternal law is that there is no light without shade, no beauty without ugliness, no white without black, for the absolute can only exist as two gods: darkness being necessary to the statue, and the brake to the locomotive. Thus, the doctrine of Satanism is a heresy; and the true and pure philosophical religion is the belief in Lucifer, the equal of Adonay; but Lucifer, God of Light and God of Good, is struggling for humanity against Adonay, the God of Darkness and Evil.

Therefore, there seems to be some indication that in the advanced degrees in Scottish Rite Freemasonry there is a focused religious sense beyond a general belief in a deity. Most Masons never progress beyond the third degree in their local Blue Lodge, but some do progress toward these upper degrees. It is perhaps interesting that the headquarters of the Scottish Rite of Freemasonry founded by Albert Pike is a few blocks from the White House, among other grand buildings of the federal government of the United States.

In 1738, only twenty-one years after Freemasonry started in London, Pope Clement XII wrote in his bull *In eminenti*: "[Freemasons] are to be condemned and prohibited, and by Our present Constitution, valid forever, We do condemn and prohibit them."[173]

[173] Clement XII, Bull on the Condemnation of Freemasonry *In eminenti* (April 28, 1738).

Beyond this condemnation, a very specific command is given to the faithful, with the penalty of excommunication attached to it:

> Wherefore We command most strictly and in virtue of holy obedience, all the faithful of whatever state, grade, condition, order, dignity or pre-eminence, whether clerical or lay, secular or regular, even those who are entitled to specific and individual mention, that none, under any pretext or for any reason, shall dare or presume to enter, propagate or support these aforesaid societies of Liberi Muratori or Francs Massons, or however else they are called, or to receive them in their houses or dwellings or to hide them, be enrolled among them, joined to them, be present with them, give power or permission for them to meet elsewhere, to help them in any way, to give them in any way advice, encouragement or support either openly or in secret, directly or indirectly, on their own or through others; nor are they to urge others or tell them, incite or persuade them to be enrolled in such societies or to be counted among their number, or to be present or to assist them in any way; but they must stay completely clear of such Societies, Companies, Assemblies, Meetings, Congregations or Conventicles, under pain of excommunication for all the above mentioned people, which is incurred by the very deed without any declaration being required, and from which no one can obtain the benefit of absolution, other than at the hour of death, except through Ourselves or the Roman Pontiff of the time.

In 1751, Pope Benedict XIV wrote in his bull *Providas Romanorum* regarding *In Eminen*: "We confirm, strengthen, renew that constitution ... we will and decree that it have perpetual force and efficacy."[174]

Pope Benedict XIV condemned Freemasonry because of its secrecy, demand for oaths, religious indifferentism, and possible threat to the Church and state. He specifically forbade Roman Catholics from seeking membership in any Masonic group.

In 1821, Pope Pius VII promulgated *Ecclesiam a Jesu Christo*, launching a papal excommunication for members of the Carbonari. The Carbonari were a group under the Freemasons, one of many revolutionary groups at the me in Italy. Pope Pius VII describes them as

> a multitude of wicked men ... united against God and Christ, with the principal aim of attacking and destroying the Church ... deceiving the faithful, and leading them astray from the doctrine of the Church by means of a vain and wicked philosophy.[175]

In 1826, Pope Leo XII wrote in *Quo graviora* regarding Freemasonry:

> Truly that abominable oath ... which must be sworn even in that lower echelon, is sufficient for you to understand that it is contrary to Divine Law to be enlisted in those lower degrees, and to remain in them.[176]

In 1829, Pope Pius VII wrote in *Traditi humilitati* regarding the religious indifferentism of Freemasonry:

[174] Benedict XIV, Bull *Providas Romanorum* (March 18, 1751).

[175] Pius VII, Bull *Ecclesiam a Jesu Christo* (September 13, 1821).

[176] Leo XII, Encyclical on Secret Societies *Quo graviora* (March 13, 1826), no. 7.

> Among these heresies ... who do not admit of any difference among the different professions of faith and who think that the portal of eternal salvation opens for all from any religion.[177]

In 1832, Pope Gregory XVI also focused on the religious indifferentism of Freemasonry in *Mirari vos*:

> This perverse opinion is spread ... that *it is possible to obtain the eternal salvation of the soul by the profession of any kind of religion.*[178]

Pope Pius IX wrote five papal bulls condemning Freemasonry. In 1846, he characterized the Masonic movement in *Qui pluribus* as "a very bitter and fearsome war against the whole Catholic commonwealth."[179]

In 1884, Pope Leo XIII wrote his encyclical *Humanum genus*, a twelve-page document devoted to condemning Freemasonry. He characterized Freemasonry in the following way:

> Its followers, joined together by a wicked compact and by secret counsels, give help to one another, and excite one another to an audacity for evil things.[180]

In 1917, the first Code of Canon Law was codified. Canon 2335 reads:

[177] Pius VII, Encyclical on His Program for His Pontificate *Traditi Humilitati* (May 24, 1829), no. 4.

[178] Gregory XVI, Encyclical on Liberalism and Religious Indifferentism *Mirari vos* (August 15, 1832), no. 13.

[179] Pius IX, Encyclical on Faith and Religion *Qui pluribus* (November 9, 1846), no. 4.

[180] Leo XIII, Encyclical on Freemasonry *Humanum genus* (April 20, 1884), no. 37.

> Those who lend their names to a Masonic sect or other association of the same kind who plot against the Church incur the penalty of excommunication resting simply in the Apostolic See.

By examining the statements of the popes, as well as the canon law of the Church, we see a clear condemnation of Freemasonry over a 245-year period starting shortly after its formation.

Indeed, we see the papal view of Freemasonry becoming clearer and more explicit in condemning the organization as being at war with the Church and inherently evil.

In more recent decades, there was a change in most lodges of Freemasonry, particularly outside of Europe. Many seemed to no longer plot against the Church, nor seemed to address the Church in any particular way. When the Code of Canon Law of 1983 came out, it combined with the public perception that Freemasons were a social club for men, and led to some confusion among Catholics. Could Catholics become Freemasons? Was the penalty of excommunication still in place? Since their lodges did not actively plot against the Church, many assumed that Freemasonry was no longer forbidden.

In 1974, The Congregation for the Doctrine of the Faith promulgated the Declaration Concerning Status of Catholics Becoming Freemasons. In it, the Congregation writes:

1. The present canonical discipline remains in full force and has not been modified in any way.
2. Consequently, neither the excommunication nor the other penalties envisaged have been abrogated.[181]

[181] Congregation for the Doctrine of the Faith, Declaration Concerning Status of Catholics Becoming Freemasons (February 17, 1981).

In 1983, the second Code of Canon Law was promulgated by Pope St. John Paul II, thereby abrogating the 1917 Code of Canon Law. The 1983 Code of Canon Law does not name Freemasonry, as the 1917 Code does. The canon that may apply is 1374:

> A person who joins an association which plots against the Church is to be punished with a just penalty; however, a person who promotes or directs an association of this kind is to be punished with an interdict.[182]

An interdict is a ban that prohibits a person from participating in Church rites, such as Communion, burial, or Marriage.

The question arose once again about the status of Freemasons. The Vatican set a number of bishops the task to study the question. They studied Freemasonry beliefs, rituals, and activities extensively. They concluded that Freemasonry is still incompatible with being Catholic.

A statement was released from the Congregation for the Doctrine of the Faith on November 26, 1983, based on this study, titled Declaration on Masonic Associations. In it, then-Cardinal Ratzinger writes,

> Therefore the Church's negative judgment in regard to Masonic association remains unchanged since their principles have always been considered irreconcilable with the doctrine of the Church and therefore membership in them remains forbidden. The faithful who enroll in

[182] CIC, c. 1374, English trans. by Vatican, https://www.vatican.va/archive/cod-iuris-canonici/eng/documents/cic_lib6-cann1364-1399_en.html#TITLE_II.

> Masonic association are in a state of grave sin and may not receive Holy Communion.[183]

So, between the 1974 declaration and the clarification in 1983, it is clearly understood that Catholic Freemasons are excommunicated from the Church, and that Catholics who become Freemasons are excommunicated from the Church.

One of the Church's stated objections to freemasonry is religious indifferentism. The Freemasons do not require a belief in Jesus Christ or His Church, yet claim to provide the mechanism of salvation. The Church has condemned indifferentism as heresy because it goes against revelation and reason. Pope Pius VIII states in *Traditi Humilitati* (1829):

> This deadly idea concerning the lack of difference among religions is refuted even by the light of natural reason. We are assured of this because the various religions do not often agree among themselves. If one is true, the other must be false; there can be no society of darkness with light.

Vatican II said there is some truth in all religions, and the Church has said that human reason is capable of finding God on its own. It has not said that all religions are equally helpful to man in this process.

When one starts from the position that all religions are equally valid, syncretism naturally follows. Syncretism is the blending of beliefs and practices from different religions. Masonic rituals draw from many religions, and extensively from Christianity, Judaism,

[183] Congregation for the Doctrine of the Faith, Declaration on Masonic Associations (November 26, 1983).

and Islam. They borrow vestments, rituals, and language from all of these religions.

The main conception of God in Freemasonry is that of deism, focusing on the Great Architect of the Universe who is worshiped in all religions. For the Mason, the observable proof of God's existence is in geometry. This is why their primary symbol for God is a G, which stands for "God, Geometry, and Gnosis." This is a necessary consequence of uniting many types of worship: to unite the worshiped. All of the prayers said to God in lodges omit the name of Jesus, instead addressing the Great Architect.

Another repeated objection to Freemasonry is their secrecy and oaths. At the first initiation into Freemasonry, into the first degree, a few notable things occur. The candidate must agree that he is offering himself freely as a "candidate for the mysteries of Freemasonry." He then must strip to his underwear and don special Masonic clothing. His is required to remove any religious symbols so that he might "carry nothing offensive of defensive into the lodge." He is then blindfolded, and a noose is placed around his neck. The junior deacon speaks for him, saying, "Mr. _____, who has long been in darkness, and now seeks to be brought to the light."

Later, in initiation to all three initial degrees of Freemasonry, there is an oath taken. Valid oaths, such as a Marriage or Holy Orders, are made publicly. These secret oaths are not valid, as they are taken in private. They incur an obligation that is lifelong. The penalty agreed to if the candidate violates his oath of secrecy at the first degree is:

> Of having my throat cut across, my tongue torn out, and with my body buried in the sands of the sea at low-water mark, where the tide ebbs and flows twice in twenty-four

> hours, should I ever knowingly or willfully violate this, my solemn Obligation of an Entered Apprentice. So help me God and make me steadfast to keep and perform the same.

The penalty for the second degree is:

> Of having my left breast torn open, my heart plucked out and placed on the highest pinnacle of the temple, there to be devoured by the vultures of the air, should I ever knowingly violate this, my Fellow Craft obligation. So help me God and keep me steadfast in the due performance of the same.

The penalty for the third degree is:

> Of having my body severed in twain, my bowels taken thence and burned to ashes, the ashes scattered to the four winds of heaven, that no more remembrance might be had of so vile a wretch as I should be to knowingly violate this, my Master Mason obligation. So help me God and keep me steadfast in the due performance of the same.

These oaths are curses called upon oneself, which are requested to be administered to the candidate by God, not man. If these oaths are not meant to be taken seriously, we may ask: Why are they sworn before God? One might also consider whether these illicit oaths are a violation of the second commandment.

It is clear that the Church has condemned Freemasonry for Catholics, and it is clear that she has, and had, good grounds to do so. Freemasonry is a deistic and syncretistic religion that removes Jesus Christ and offers its own route to heaven without him. It requires the divesting of religious symbols and the calling down of grotesque curses from God on oneself in secret invalid oaths. Finally, Freemasonry emerged from the intellectual climate of the Reformation and Enlightenment, and historically sought to attack and harm the Church as an institution. In addition to these issues seen in the first three degrees of Freemasonry, we find hints about a more explicitly Satanic or Luciferian mindset in the Scottish Rite as expressed by the "father" of that order, Albert Pike.

For the three hundred years of Freemasonry's existence, the Church's position on it has been clear. There was a brief period of public confusion about this, which the Church corrected authoritatively. Catholics cannot be, or become, Freemasons without incurring the punishment of excommunication.

The history and Freemasonry and the Church being reviewed we can now return to 1890, a time when the Church was subject to significant political and social persecution, which was being fomented by her greatest enemy, Freemasonry.

The Exorcism Rite of Pope Leo XIII in 1890

In 1890, Pope Leo XIII (1878–1903) added an appendix to the 1614 exorcism rite, his *Exorcism against Satan and the Apostate Angels* (referred to as the Minor Exorcism of 1890 hereafter). We will see later that this rite of exorcism was modified and included as the second chapter of the 1998 *Exorcisms and Related Supplications*. Some verifiable facts, and much unverifiable legend, exist about the creation of the Minor Exorcism of 1890. A well-researched book on that topic is available.[184]

[184] K. Symonds, *Pope Leo XIII and the Prayer to Saint Michael* (Boonville, NY: Preserving Christian, 2015).

There is one rubric and one footnote in the Minor Exorcism of 1890. The rubric is:

> The following exorcism can be used by bishops, as well as by priests who have this authorization from their Ordinary.

This is essentially identical to the restriction on the use of the exorcism rite of 1614. The footnote reads:

> Whereas the preceding rite of exorcism is designated for a particular person, the form given here is meant especially to be employed to expel the devil's sway over a locality [parish, city, etc.].

There has been considerable violation of the rubric for the Minor Exorcism of 1890, in the form of laypeople using it. Instances occurred where the rubric was removed and the rite disseminated online without it. In some cases, laypeople were encouraged to use it. When laypeople use this rite it is illicit and invalid, as they no not have permission, and they do not have the priestly faculty necessary to use the rite if they had permission.

Exorcism in the 1917 Code of Canon Law

The 1917 Code of Canon Law has three canons (1151–1153) related to exorcism:

> *Canon 1151*
>
> §1. No one, even if endowed with the power of exorcism, can legitimately perform an exorcism over the [possessed] unless he has obtained express and specific authorization from the Ordinary.

§2. This authorization from the Ordinary can be granted only to priests outstanding for piety, prudence, and integrity of life; such a one shall not proceed to exorcism unless, after a diligent and prudent investigation, he finds that the one to be exorcised is actually [possessed] by a demon.

Canon 1152

Exorcisms by legitimate ministers can be performed not only on the faithful and catechumens, but also upon non-Catholics and the excommunicated.

Canon 1153

The ministers of the exorcisms that occur in baptism and in consecrations or blessings are those who are the legitimate ministers of those sacred rites.[185]

Canon 1151 §1 echoes item 1 in the *praenotanda* of the 1614 rite of exorcism. It separates possessing the faculty of exorcism (which creates validity), which came from ordination to the minor order of exorcist at that time, from legitimate permission to use that faculty (which creates liceity).[186] Canon 1151 §2 also derives from the same, and from item 3

[185] CIC 17, cc. 1151–1153, English trans. in E. Peters, ed., *The 1917 Pio-Benedictine Code of Canon Law* (San Francisco: Ignatius Press, 2001), p. 394.

[186] See, e.g., J. Paschang, "The Sacramentals According to the Code of Canon Law" (Ph.D. diss., Catholic University of America, 1925), p. 100; see C. Bachofen, *A Commentary on the New Code of Canon Law*, third rev. ed., bk. 3, vol. 4 (St. Louis, MO: Herder, 1925), p. 569.

in the *praenotanda* of the 1614 rite. Only priests, and not those only ordained with the minor order of exorcist were allowed to perform exorcisms. Previous to this, clerics with only the minor order were allowed to perform exorcisms of people.[187] The priest must reach moral certitude before proceeding to an exorcism.[188] Canon 1152 addresses a presumption built into the 1614 rite that the energumen is Catholic and has access to the sacraments. A sacramental is normally seen as a preparation for participation in the sacraments, but this canon broadens the conception of exorcism and charitably allows broader use. Canon 1153 separates the exorcism of energumens from the exorcism of the catechumens in preparation for Baptism, or the other places in the Church rite that have exorcism built in (Baptism, RCIA). It also clarifies the potential misunderstanding that only the diocesan exorcist can do any of the lesser exorcisms in other Church rites.

Exorcism and Vatican II

The Second Vatican Council (Vatican II from here on) promulgated *Sacrosanctum concilium* on December 4, 1963. Article 79 states:

> The sacramentals are to be revised, account being taken of the primary principle of enabling the faithful to

[187] H. Ayrinhac, *Legislation on the Sacraments in the New Code of Canon Law* (New York: Longmans and Green, 1928), p. 405.

[188] Paschang, "The Sacramentals According to the Code of Canon Law," pp. 104–105; T. Bouscaren and A. Ellis, *Canon Law: A Text and Commentary*, 3rd rev. ed. (Milwaukee: Bruce, 1957), p. 633.

> participate intelligently, actively, and easily. The circumstances of our times must also be considered. When rituals are being revised as laid down in Article 63, new sacramentals may also be added as necessity requires.[189]

This requirement for revision applied to exorcism, as it is a sacramental.

Pope Paul VI (1963–1978) oversaw much of the implementation of Vatican II. He removed the minor order of exorcist (and three other minor orders) by his moto proprio *Ministeria quaedam*.[190] This made sense as the order of exorcist had been obsolete since the 1917 Code of Canon Law limited the use of the rite to priests. Interestingly, he left the door open for episcopal conferences to request that this order be restored in their region:

> In addition to the offices common to the Latin Church, nothing prevents episcopal conferences from petitioning the Apostolic See for others whose institution in their region, for special reasons, they judge to be necessary or very useful. To those, for example, belong the offices of porter, exorcist and catechist.[191]

[189] Vatican Council II, Dogmatic Constitution on the Sacred Liturgy *Sacrosanctum concilium* (December 4, 1963), no. 79, English trans. in *Flannery 1*, p. 23.

[190] Paul VI, Motu Proprio on First Tonsure, Minor Orders, and the Subdiaconate *Ministeria quaedam* (August 15, 1972), in *AAS* 64 (1972): p. 531, English trans. in *CLD* 7 (1975): p. 692.

[191] Paul VI, *Ministeria quaedam*.

The 1983 Code of Canon Law and Exorcism

The 1983 Code of Canon Law was promulgated by Pope St. John Paul II on January 25, 1983.[192] Canon 1172 addresses exorcism of energumens:

> §1. No one can perform exorcisms legitimately upon the possessed unless he has obtained special and express permission from the local ordinary.
>
> §2. The local ordinary is to give this permission only to a presbyter who has piety, knowledge, prudence, and integrity of life.[193]

The code only addresses who can do exorcisms of the possessed, and under what circumstances. The other rules are left to the instructions in the *Roman Ritual*. It is interesting to note that the word *presbyter* is used, which excludes bishops being able to do exorcisms. The 1917 Code used the word *sacerdoti* in the Latin, which includes both priests and bishops:

> 1151 §2. Haec licentia ab Ordinario concedatur tantummodo sacerdoti pietate, prudential ac vitae intergritate praedito; qui ad exorcismos ne procedat, nisi postquam diligenti prudentique investigatione comperit exorcizandum esse revera a daemone osessum.[194]

[192] John Paul II, Apostolic Constitution for the Promulgation of the New Code of Canon Law *Sacrae disciplinae leges* (January 25, 1983), in *AAS* 75, part 2 (1983): pp. vi–xiv.

[193] CIC, c. 1172, English trans. in *Code of Canon Law, Latin-English Edition, New English Translation* (Washington, DC: CLSA, 1999), p. 365.

[194] CIC 17 (Rome: Typis Polyglottis Vaticanis 1965), p. 313.

The other important change is the addition of "local ordinary" instead of "ordinary." This excludes superiors of religious institutes and societies of apostolic life, as defined in paragraph 2 of canon 134:

> §2. By the title of local ordinary are understood all those mentioned in §1 except the superiors of religious institutes and of societies of apostolic life.[195]

Non-Catholics and the excommunicated are not mentioned in the 1983 code. Canon 1331 bars the excommunicated from receiving sacraments, and celebrating the sacraments and sacramentals.[196] This does not bar them from *receiving* sacramentals. Baptized non-Catholics are also not barred from receiving sacramentals in canon law.

The 1998 Rite of Exorcism

The Congregation for Divine Worship and Discipline of the Sacraments (CDWDS) promulgated the revised rite of exorcism on November 22, 1998.[197] By canon 20 of the 1983 code, this abrogated the old rite.[198] It was published in a book in 1999 that contains the rite for possessed people and for locations (essentially a revised Minor Exorcism of 1890), and prayers that

[195] CIC, c. 134, English trans. in *Code of Canon Law, Latin-English Edition, New English Translation*, p. 39.

[196] CIC, c. 1331 §2, English trans. in *Code of Canon Law, Latin-English Edition, New English Translation*, p. 417.

[197] CDWDS, Decree *Inter sacramentalia* (November 22, 1998), in *Notitiae* 35 (1999): p. 137.

[198] CIC, c. 20, English trans. in *Code of Canon Law, Latin-English Edition, New English Translation*, p. 10.

the faithful can use in an appendix. This initial edition was not widely circulated, nor officially translated into any languages from the Latin, except Italian. The rite underwent a number of revisions. Some of the text, as well as the addition of an appendix that contains many of the more imprecatory and combative language that was not used in this rite (but played a prominent role in the 1614 rite). The number of revisions is not published, but the commonly discussed number in the exorcist community is five.[199] The edition that was finally published by the USCCB, in an English translation, had a first printing in 2017.

The *praenotanda* of the 1998 rite is divided into six sections, which are summarized here:[200]

1: The Victory of Christ and the Power of the Church against Demons

This is a theological summary of Catholic cosmology and the history of salvation, with an emphasis on Christ defeating the demons in exorcisms, and Satan by the Cross. Christ gave authority to the Church over demons, and commanded the Church to perform exorcisms as He had demonstrated. The Church, since earliest times, has obeyed this command.

2: Exorcisms in the Church's Office of Sanctifying

The exorcism of the catechumens is defined as *minor exorcism* and helps free the catechumens from the influence of the devil, while they prepare for Baptism. The faithful are encouraged to avoid

[199] The author has been involved in the training of exorcists in the United States since 2005 and knows many of the exorcists in the country.

[200] USCCB, *Exorcisms and Related Supplications*, pp. 3–10.

sin and participate in the Sacrament of Penance. Oppression and possession happen and are allowed by God. When they occur, the Church offers the faithful a number of remedies. Chief among these is the major exorcism, also called "great," which is a liturgical action. The Church acts in the name of God or Christ the Lord, not in her own name.

3: The Minister and Conditions for Performing a Major Exorcism

Exorcism ministry is done by a priest, with special and express permission of the local ordinary, who as a rule is the diocesan bishop. The appointee should be endowed with piety, knowledge, prudence, and integrity of life. He should also be specifically prepared for this office. He should act with confidence and humility. He should be very careful to have moral certainty the person is possessed, and not quickly judge. If he has reached moral certainty, he should have the consent of the energumen before doing an exorcism. Many people think that they are under a demonic affliction because of bad luck, this should not be treated with exorcism. The signs of possession are: facility in languages not known to the person, knowledge of hidden things, abnormal strength, and vehement aversion to the holy. The exorcist should consult experts in medicine and science, if necessary. Cases of non-Catholics should be brought to the bishop's attention for his decision on the matter. Exorcism should never be treated as a magical or superstitious action. Media or recording of any kind is forbidden, and confidentiality should be observed by all.

4: The Rite to Be Used

The rite involves the Sign of the Cross, the imposition of hands, the breathing upon, and the sprinkling of holy water. Holy water is used at the outset as a reminder of the Baptism of the energumen. Then the Litany of the Saints is prayed, followed by a number of psalms. The Gospel is proclaimed, and then the exorcist imposes his hands on the energumen and invokes the Holy Spirit to free the person from the demon. He may also breathe on the person at this time. The Apostles' Creed is recited, the person renews his baptismal promises, and the Lord's Prayer is said. The person is shown the Cross, and the Sign of the Cross is made over them. Then the priest says the deprecatory exorcism prayers and finally the imprecatory exorcism prayers. All of the preceding can be repeated. The rite is concluded with a canticle of thanksgiving, a prayer, and a blessing.

5: Circumstances and Accommodations

The exorcist, and his team, if possible, should fast and pray for the freedom of the energumen. The energumen should, if possible, pray, fast, and participate in the sacraments. The exorcism should take place in a church where a crucifix is prominent and an image of Mary is displayed. There should not be outside spectators of any kind. The exorcist should encourage the energumen to trust in God, plead for freedom, and bear his suffering patiently. The exorcist's team should pray for the person during the exorcism, but never use any of the exorcism prayers. After the person is freed, he should persevere in prayer, read the Bible, and do works of charity and love toward all.

6: Adaptions within the Competence of the Conferences of Bishops

The conference of bishops is to do an accurate translation. It is also to petition to the Holy See to adapt the signs and gestures of the rite if its particular cultural sensibilities call for it. It may also add a pastoral directory on the use of a major exorcism if it chooses. This should be compiled from approved authors and cover the rite in more depth and practical detail. This can be done in collaboration with priests with long experience as exorcists, and with a *recognitio* from the Holy See affirming their expertise.

Chapter 1 follows, which is the "Rite of Major Exorcism" for the possessed, composed of the steps described above in the summary of section 4 of the *praenotanda*.

Chapter 2 is called "Various Texts Which May Optionally be Used in the Rite." This includes Psalms 3, 11(10), 13(12), 22(21), 31(30) 35(34), 54(53), 68(67), 70(69) and some short prayers of petition.

Appendix 1 is "A Supplication and Exorcism Which May be Used in Particular Circumstances of the Church." It is to be said when the bishop decides, and must be led by a priest, but not necessarily an exorcist priest. The imprecatory prayer section has a rubric that it may only be said by the priest. Some of the other prayers the faithful respond to, or join in saying with the priest, as directed by the rubrics. It contains a number of prayers of petition, and a section of imprecatory commands made by the exorcist, and concludes with part of the St. Michael prayers from the minor exorcism of Pope Leo XIII.

Appendix 2 is "Supplications which may be Used by the Faithful Privately in Their Struggle Against the Powers of Darkness." There are no restrictions on who can use these prayers. The only rubric is at the Sign of the Cross: the faithful may "appropriately sign themselves with the Sign of the Cross." This section includes prayers of petition, invocations to the Most Holy Trinity, invocations to Our Lord Jesus Christ, invocations to the Blessed Virgin Mary, and invocations to St. Michael the archangel.

Changes in Law after the Promulgation of the 1998 Rite of Exorcism

The 1998 rite of exorcism was approved by Pope St. John Paul II on October 1, 1998. On the next day, he granted the CDWDS a special faculty to permit the use of the former rite by a priest on whose behalf his bishop had requested this permission.[201]

Pope Benedict XVI promulgated his moto proprio *Summorum pontificum* on July 17, 2007. While it primarily allowed for the celebration of the Latin Mass in the Roman Missal promulgated by Pope St. John XXIII in 1962, article 9 addressed other sacraments and the Roman Breviary:[202]

> §1. The parish priest, after careful consideration, can also grant permission to use the older ritual in the administration of the sacraments of Baptism, Marriage, Penance and Anointing of the Sick, if advantageous for the good of souls.
>
> §2. Ordinaries are granted the faculty of celebrating the sacrament of Confirmation using the old Roman Pontifical, if advantageous for the good of souls.
>
> §3. Ordained clerics may also use the Roman Breviary promulgated in 1962 by Blessed John XXIII.

This was interpreted by the Pontifical Commission Ecclesia Dei on April 30, 2011, in their Instruction on the Application

[201] CDWDS, Notification *De ritu exorcismi* (January 27, 1999), in *Notitiae* 35 (1999): p. 156.

[202] Benedict XVI, Motu Proprio on the Use of the Roman Liturgy Prior to the Reform of 1970 *Summorum pontificum* (July 17, 2007).

of the Apostolic Letter *Summorum Pontificum* of his Holiness Benedict XVI Given *Motu Proprio*. Part of that interpretation allowed for the use of the entire *Rituale Romanum* of 1962:

> The use of the *Pontificale Romanum*, the *Rituale Romanum*, as well as the *Caeremoniale Episcoporum* in effect in 1962, is permitted, in keeping with n. 28 of this Instruction, and always respecting n. 31 of the same Instruction.[203]

This allowed for the use of the 1614 rite of exorcism, part of the *Rituale Romanum* of 1962, without special permission.

Pope Francis abrogated *Summorum pontificum* on July 16, 2021, with his motu proprio *Traditionis custodes*. He addressed a number of points related to the celebration of the Latin Mass. Article 8 abrogated *Summorum pontificum*:

> Previous norms, instructions, permissions, and customs that do not conform to the provisions of the present *Motu Proprio* are abrogated.[204]

Since the previous permissions and instructions about the solemn exorcism were not related to the Latin Mass, they remain in force: the use of the 1614 rite of exorcism is still allowed without special permission. In practice, most bishops allow their exorcists to use whichever rite they are more comfortable with or prefer to use. That being said, there have been questions that were debated in the past, and a future *dubia* (official question to Rome) may yield a different interpretation of the law.

[203] Pontifical Commission Ecclesia Dei, Instruction on the Application of the Apostolic Letter *Summorum Pontificum* of his Holiness Benedict XVI Given *Motu Proprio* (April 30, 2011), no. 35.

[204] Francis, Motu Proprio on the Use of the Roman Liturgy Prior to the Reform of 1970 *Traditionis custodes* (July 16, 2021), no. 8.

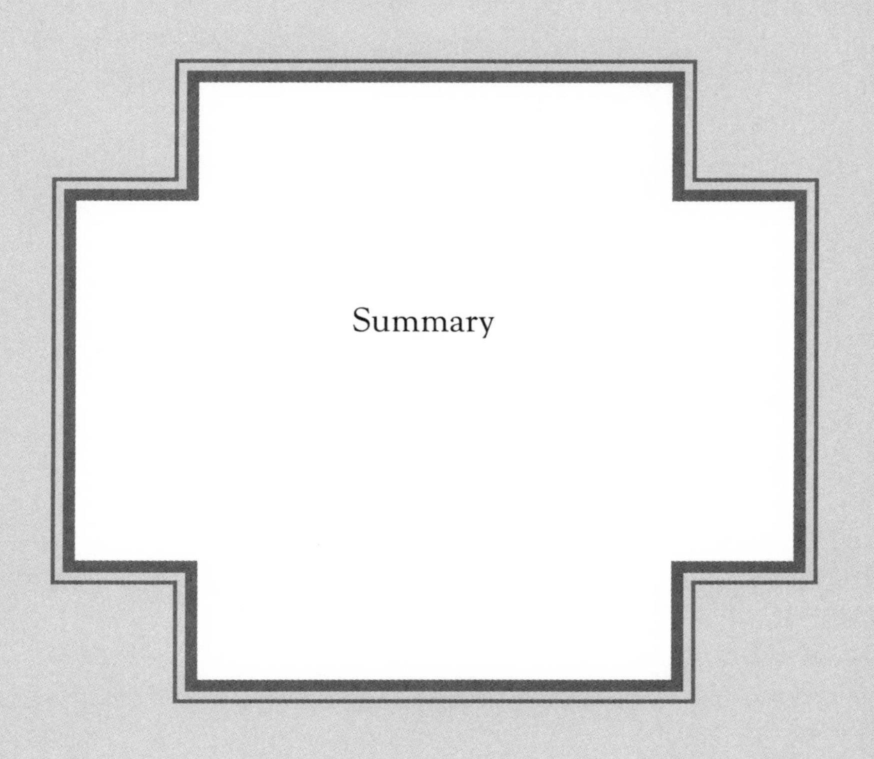

Summary

+

The laws of the Church governing exorcism developed in order to address three questions: What is a solemn exorcism, who can perform it, and whom can they perform it on? The law addressing these three questions developed over the past two millennia of Church history. The three places the law currently speaks on exorcism are in canon 1172 of the 1983 Code of Canon Law, the *praenotanda* of the 1614 rite, and the *praenotanda* of the 1998 rite. There may also be local laws in some bishops' conferences or dioceses.

A solemn exorcism as a fixed rite of the Church developed in the decades leading up to 1614. Before then, the act of exorcising a person was not universally formulaic, and it was regulated by law to varying degrees depending on location and time. The rite of 1614 defines the text to be read and actions to be taken, as well as a few items used during the exorcism (a crucifix, the purple stole, and holy water). It allows some room for the exorcist to interrogate the demon in a freeform manner, but the information sought is limited to what the rite allows (the demon's name, how it entered the person, and the date and hour appointed for its departure).

The 1998 rite of exorcism directs fewer words to the demon and instead directs most words to God. Similar interrogation to the 1614 rite is allowed. The 1614 rite of exorcism uses a significant amount of words, and direct commands, to the demon, while the new rite prefers to request that the Holy Spirit exorcise the demon. A large part of the appeal to the Holy Spirit is based on the presence of baptismal graces. Solemn exorcism in both rites is not done in public view; rather, it is always done confidentially and with approved witnesses.

Since the 1614 rite of exorcism, it has been the universal law of the Church that only a priest with permission from his bishop can perform solemn exorcisms on people. That permission is express and special, and so is on a case-by-case basis. Deacons cannot perform solemn exorcisms, and certainly laity cannot either. In the ancient Church, there were laypeople, often hermits or other devout religious, that performed exorcisms by the Sign of the Cross or the invocation of the name of Jesus. Today these actions would not be called a solemn exorcism, but private deliverance prayer.

Today the Church responds to requests for exorcism from adults, or in rare cases from the parents of people under the age of adulthood. She does not do exorcisms on adults at the request of third parties. She responds with an investigation of the case that involves outside medical and psychological evaluation. Then she investigates for the signs that lead to moral certainty that a demon is possessing the person. The exorcist must have this moral certainty, and present the proofs to the bishop, in order to seek approval to use the rite of exorcism. Those proofs include facility in languages the person does not know, knowledge of things the person has no way of knowing, reactions to the holy, and strength beyond the person's condition in life.

Summary

While there have not been frequent changes in the law regulating exorcism, this is not a bad thing. This implies that the time-tested laws of the Church have been effective and helpful in most ages. As the Church, and the world, renew interest in exorcism there is a need to revisit it in our modern context. The rite was recently revised, but the three questions are still answered in the same way. The Church seeks to provide remedy for those suffering under demonic affliction, protect the safety and dignity of those people, and protect her priests and institutions from harms that can arise from confronting embodied demons.

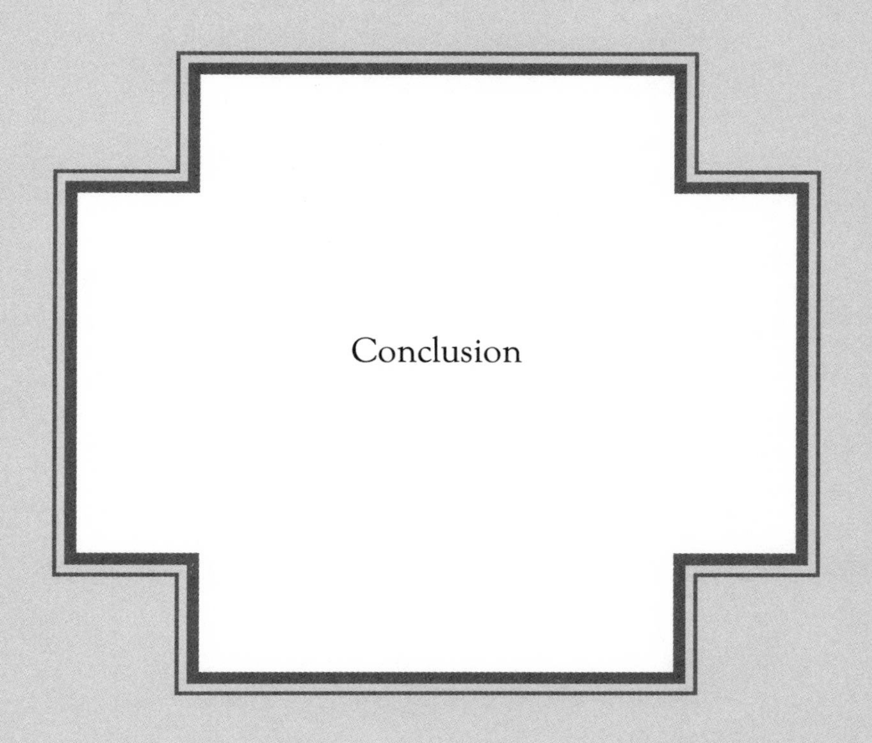

Conclusion

✠

There has been a resurgence of exorcism ministry in the Church, and particularly in the United States, at the beginning of the 21st century. Where there used to be few exorcists scattered across the nation there are now well more than a hundred. Where there used to only be limited training available in Rome, there is a burgeoning school of exorcism in Chicago. Where there used to be no meetings for mutual support, there are national conferences, retreats, and personal training. Where there was minimal information available to the public there are books, YouTube videos, and interviews from a number of exorcists. Where there used to be no training in seminary, there are workshops and classes to teach parish priests how to deal with the lesser demonic problems in their parishes on their own. Where exorcism was misunderstood, and sometimes feared, there is open discussion in the Church and media that has made it almost commonplace.

The West seems endlessly fascinated by this ancient ministry. Perhaps it is because demons are so well established in the mind of the West. Perhaps it is because it is a place where the curtain is pulled back and the spiritual is there to see, touch, and hear. More likely it is because there is an innate, instinctual response to demons, something in us that says 'that is real, that is dangerous' in spite of our personal thoughts on the matter. Whatever the reason, the interest in the people doing this work, and the cases they have seen, seems to never wane.

The information that makes it to the average person through the filter of the media is always incomplete, and often misunderstood. It is analogous to watching an interview with a surgeon here or there and then assuming you are ready to perform surgery. It takes a lot of background understanding of theology and the Church to fully understand what is happening in an exorcism. It also takes a lot of understanding of people and how their thinking and lives can be distorted by the trauma of being possessed for years. Undoing a possession is a lot more than reading some pages from a book. It is working with the person to understand them and how they got into trouble. It is dealing with the demon's distractions, attacks, lies, and manipulation. It is praying from the heart for hours while being verbally and physically abused by the demons. Most importantly, it is about truly trusting Jesus with your life, and eventually seeing the miracle of Him free that person.

This ministry is simultaneously hard and effortless. It is hard on the human level, but the yoke is light when we realize Jesus is doing all the work. He made us, He drew us into ministry, He protects us, and He does the exorcisms. Yes, the Church prays, but without God acting through His church, nothing would happen. We who work in this area are just doing our part in the mystical body of Christ, which is His church. The Church, as we have seen, is doing her part to guide and protect us.

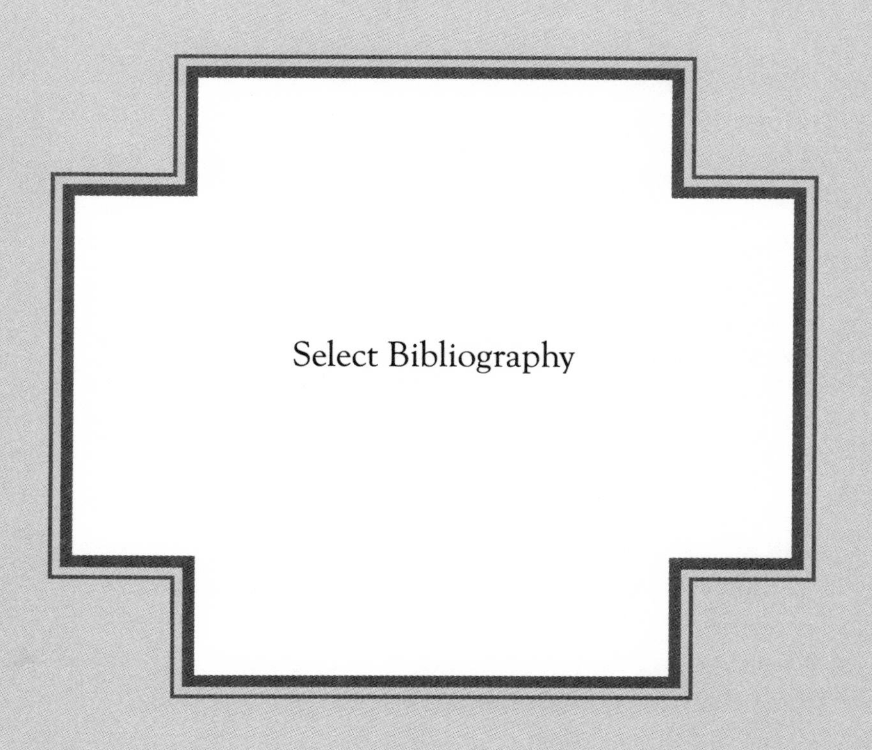

Select Bibliography

✠

Church Sources

Acta Apostolicae Sedis, Rome, 1909–.

Acta et Decreta Sacrorum Conciliorum Recentiorum: Collectio Lacensis. 7 vols. Friburgi Brisgoviae: Herder, 1870–1892.

Benedict XVI. Motu Proprio on the Use of the Roman Liturgy Prior to the Reform of 1970, *Summorum pontificum*. July 17, 2007.

CDWDS. Decree *De exorcismis et supplicationibus quibusdam, editio typica emendata*. Rome: Typis Polyglottis Vaticanis, 2004.

——. Decree *De exorcismis et supplicationibus quibusdam, editio typica*. Rome: Typis Polyglottis Vaticanis, 1999.

——. Notification *De ritu exorcismi*. January 27, 1999. In *Notitiae* 35 (1999): p. 156.

——. Decree *Inter sacramentalia*. November 22, 1998. In *Notitiae* 35 (1999): p. 137.

Codex Iuris Canonici, auctoritate Ioannis Pauli PP. II promulgatus fontium annotatione et indice analytico-alphabetico auctus, Libreria editrice Vaticana, 1989. English translation *Code of Canon Law, Latin-English Edition, New English Translation*. Washington, DC: CLSA, 1999.

Codex Iuris Canonici, Pii X Pontificis Maximi iussu digestus Benedicti Papae XV auctoritate promulgatus. New York: P. J. Kennedy, 1918.

Codex Iuris Canonici Pii X Pontificis Maximi iussu digestus Benedicti Papae XV auctoritate promulgates. Rome: Typis Polyglottis Vaticanis, 1917. English translation in *The 1917 Pio-Benedictine Code of Canon Law*, ed. E. Peters. San Francisco: Ignatius Press, 2001.

Congregation for the Doctrine of the Faith. *Christian Faith and Demonology*. June 26, 1975. In *La Documentation Catholique* 72 (1975): pp. 708–718. English translation in *The Pope Speaks* 20 (1975).

——. Instruction on Prayers for Healing *Instructio de orationibus ad obtinendam a deo sanationem*. September 14, 2000. In *Notitiae* 37 (2001): pp. 20–34. English translation in *Notitiae* 37 (2001): pp. 51–65.

——. Letter *Inde ab aliquot annis*. September 29, 1984. In *AAS* 11 (1985): pp. 1169–1170. English translation in *CLD* 11 (1991): pp. 276–277.

Gasparri, P., ed. *Codicis iuris canonici fontes*. 9 vols. Rome: Typis Polyglottis Vaticanis, 1926–1939.

John Paul II. Apostolic Constitution for the Promulgation of the New Code of Canon Law *Sacrae disciplinae leges*. January 25, 1983. In *AAS* 15, part 2 (1983): pp. vi–xiv.

——. General Audience. August 13, 1986.

Paul V. Apostolic Constitution *Apostolicae sedi*. June 17, 1614. In *Codicis iuris canonici fontes*, ed. P. Gasparri, vol. 1, pp. 378–379. Rome: Typis Polyglottis Vaticanis, 1926.

Paul VI. Motu Proprio on First Tonsure, Minor Orders, and the Subdiaconate *Ministeria quaedam*. August 15, 1972. In

AAS 64 (1972): pp. 529–534. English translation in *CLD* 7 (1975): pp. 690–695.

"Prefect for Divine Worship on the New Rite of Exorcism." EWTN. January 26, 1999. Accessed March 13, 2023. https://www.ewtn.com/catholicism/library/prefect-for-divine-worship-on-the-new-rite-of-exorcism-4275.

Rituale Romanum: Editio Princeps (1614). Edited by M. Sodi and J. Arcas. Vatican City: Libreria Editrice Vaticana, 2004.

Rituale Romanum: Pauli V Pontificis Maximi jussu editum. Rome: Typis Polyglottis Vaticanis, 1957.

Rituale Romanum: Reimpressio editionis primae post typicam anno 1953 publici iuris factae, textibus postea approbatis, introductione et tabulis aucta. Edited by A. Ward and C. Johnson. Rome: C. L. V.–Edizioni Liturgiche, 2001.

Roman Ritual: Complete Edition. Translated by P. Weller. Milwaukee, WI: Bruce, 1964.

Roman Ritual: In Latin and English with Rubrics and Plainchant Notation. 3 vols. Translated and edited by P. Weller. Milwaukee: Bruce, 1950–1952.

USCCB. *Exorcisms and Related Supplications*. Washington, DC: ICEL, 2017.

Sacrorum Conciliorum Nova et Amplissima Collectio. Edited by J. Mansi. 31 vols. Paris: H. Welter, 1901–1927.

Vatican Council II. Constitution on the Sacred Liturgy *Sacrosanctum concilium*. December 4, 1963. In AAS, 56 (1964): pp. 97–138. English translation in *Flannery 1*, pp. 1–36.

Books

Allen, T. B. *Possessed: The True Story of an Exorcism*. 2nd ed. Lincoln, NE: iUniverse, 2000.

Aquinas, Thomas. *Summa Theologiae*, vol. 39. Translated by K. O'Rourke, O.P. Blackfriars. London: Eyre and Spottiswoode, 1964.

——. *Summa Theologiae*, vol. 57. Translated by J. Cunningham, O.P. Blackfriars. London: Eyre and Spottiswoode, 1975.

——. *Summa Theologiae*, vol. 59. Translated by T. Gilby, O.P. Blackfriars. London: Eyre and Spottiswoode, 1975.

Athanasius. *Contra Gentes and De Incarnatione*. Translated by R. Thomson. Oxford: Clarendon Press, 1971.

——. *The Life of Antony and the Letter to Marcellinus*. Translated by R. Gregg. New York: Paulist Press, 1980.

Ayrinhac, H. *Legislation on the Sacraments in the New Code of Canon Law*. New York: Longmans and Green, 1928.

Boadt, L. *Reading the Old Testament: An Introduction*. New York: Paulist Press, 1984.

Bouscaren, T. and A. Ellis. *Canon Law: A Text and Commentary*. 3rd rev. ed. Milwaukee, WI: Bruce, 1957.

Carr, W. *Angels and Principalities: The Background, Meaning, and Development of the Pauline Phrase Hai Archai Kai Hai Exousiai*. Cambridge, MA: Cambridge University Press, 1981.

Clark, S. *Thinking with Demons: The Idea of Witchcraft in Early Modern Europe*. Oxford: Clarendon Press, 1997.

The Complete Parallel Bible: Containing the Old and New Testaments with the Apocryphal/Deuterocanonical Books. Oxford: Oxford University Press, 1993.

Coriden, J. A., T. J. Green, and D. E. Heintschel, eds. *The Code of Canon Law: A Text and Commentary*. New York: Paulist Press, 1985.

Cross, F. and E. Livingstone, eds. *The Oxford Dictionary of the Christian Church*. 3rd rev. ed. Oxford: Oxford University Press, 2005.

Davies, T. W., *Magic, Divination, and Demonology among the Hebrews and Their Neighbors*. New York: Ktav, 1969.

Eisenhofer, L. and J. Lechner. *The Liturgy of the Roman Rite*. Edited by H. Winstone. Translated by A. Peeler and E. Peeler. New York: Herder and Herder, 1961.

Epiphanius. *Panarion of St. Epiphanius, Bishop of Salamis*. Translated by P. Amidon. Oxford: Oxford University Press, 1990.

Ferber, S. *Demonic Possession and Exorcism in Early Modern France*. London: Routledge, 2004.

Ferguson, E. *Demonology of the Early Christian World*. Symposium Series 12. New York: Edwin Mellen Press, 1984.

Finlay, A. *Demons! The Devil, Possession & Exorcism*. London: Blandford, 1999.

Flannery, A., ed. *Vatican Council II*, vol. 1: *The Conciliar and Postconciliar Documents*. New rev. ed. Northport, NY: Costello, 1998.

Franz, A. *Die Kirchlichen Benediktionen im Mittelalter*. 2 vols. Graz: Akademische Druck und Verlagsanstalt, 1960.

Gelasian Sacramentary: Liber Sacramentorum Romanae Ecclesiae. Edited by H. Wilson. Oxford: Clarendon Press, 1894.

Goodman, F. D. *How about Demons? Possession and Exorcism in the Modern World*. Bloomington, IN: Indiana University Press, 1988.

The Gregorian Sacramentary under Charles the Great. Edited by H. Wilson. Henry Bradshaw Society. London: Harrison, 1915.

Hefele, C. *A History of the Councils of the Church: From the Original Documents*. Translated by H. Oxenham. 5 vols. Edinburgh: T and T Clark, 1896.

Irenaeus of Lyon, *Five Books Against Heresies*, Edited by W. Harvey, Rochester, St. Irenaeus Press, 2013.

Josephus. *Jewish Antiquities, vol. 5: Books V–VIII*. Translated by H. Thackeray and R. Marcus. Cambridge, MA: Harvard University Press, 1988.

Kee, H. *Medicine, Miracle, and Magic in New Testament Times*. Society for New Testament Studies 55. Cambridge, MA: Cambridge University Press, 1986.

Kelly, H. A. *The Devil, Demonology, and Witchcraft: The Development of Christian Beliefs in Evil Spirits*. Garden City, NY: Doubleday, 1968.

Lactantius, *Divine Institute,* Translated by A.Bowne and P. Garnsey, Liverpool, Liverpool University Press, 2004.

Landon, E. *A Manual of Councils of the Holy Catholic Church*. Rev. ed. 2 vols. Edinburgh, J. Grant: 1909.

Langton, E. *Essentials of Demonology: A Study of Jewish and Christian Doctrine, Its Origin, and Development*. Eugene, OR: Wipf and Stock, 2014.

Levack, B., ed. *Possession and Exorcism*. Articles on Witchcraft, Magic and Demonology, vol. 9. New York: Garland, 1992.

Marzoa, A., J. Miras, and R. Rodríguez-Ocaña, eds. *Exegetical Commentary on the Code of Canon Law*. English ed., ed. E. Caparros. 5 vols. Chicago, IL: Midwest Theological Forum, 2004.

Menghi, G., *The Devil's Scourge: Exorcism during the Italian Renaissance*. Edited and Translated by G. Paxia. York Beach, ME: Weiser Books, 2002.

Nyder, J. *Formicarius*. Edited by H. Biedermann. Graz: Akademische Druck und Verlagsanstalt, 1971.

Oesterreich, T. K. *Possession and Exorcism among Primitive Races in Antiquity, the Middle Ages, and Modern Times*. Translated by D. Ibberson. 1922; repr. New York: Causeway Books, 1974.

Origen. *Origen: Contra Celsum.* Translated by H. Chadwick. Cambridge, MA: Cambridge University Press, 1980.

Paschang, J. "The Sacramentals According to the Code of Canon Law." Ph.D. diss., Catholic University of America, 1925.

Rodewyk, A. *Possessed by Satan: The Church's Teaching on the Devil, Possession, and Exorcism.* Translated by M. Ebon. Garden City, NY: Doubleday, 1975.

Russell, J. *Lucifer: The Devil in the Middle Ages.* Ithaca, NY: Cornell University Press, 1984.

——. *Witchcraft in the Middle Ages.* Ithaca, NY: Cornell University Press, 1972.

Sheehy, G. and F. G. Morrisey, eds. *The Canon Law, Letter & Spirit: A Practical Guide to the Code of Canon Law.* Collegeville, MN: Liturgical Press, 1995.

Thyraeus, P. *Daemoniaci, Hoc Est: De Obsessis a Spiritibus Daemoniorum Hominibus.* Cologne: Agrippina, 1598.

Twelftree, G. *Christ Triumphant: Exorcism Then and Now.* London: Hodder and Stoughton, 1985.

——. *Jesus the Exorcist: A Contribution to the Study of the Historical Jesus.* Peabody, MA: Hendrickson, 1993.

Van Der Loos, H. *The Miracles of Jesus.* Leiden: E. J. Brill, 1965.

Vogel, C., *Medieval Liturgy: An Introduction to the Sources.* Translated by W. Storey and N. Rasmussen. Pastoral Press, 1981.

Walker, D. P., *Unclean Spirits: Possession and Exorcism in France and England in the Late Sixteenth and Early Seventeenth Centuries,* London, Scolar Press, 1981.

——. *Unclean Spirits: Possession and Exorcism in France and England in the Late Sixteenth and Early Seventeenth Centuries.* Philadelphia: University of Pennsylvania Press, 1981.

Young, F. A *History of Exorcism in Catholic Christianity.* Palgrave Mcmillian, Switzerland, 2016.

Articles and Chapters

Ericson, G. "The Enigmatic Metamorphosis: From Divine Possession to Demonic Possession." *Journal of Popular Culture* 11, no. 3 (Winter 1977): pp. 656–681.

Frankfurter, D. "Where the Spirits Dwell: Possession, Christianization, and Saints' Shrines in Late Antiquity." *Harvard Theological Review* 103, no. 1 (January 2010): pp. 27–46.

Goddu, A. "The Failure of Exorcism in the Middle Ages." In *Possession and Exorcism*, edited by B. Levack, pp. 2–20. Articles on Witchcraft, Magic and Demonology, vol. 9. New York: Garland, 1992.

Hanson, C. "The Liberty of the Bishop to Improvise Prayer in the Eucharist." *Vigiliae Christianae* 15, no. 3 (September 1961): pp. 173–176.

Hillers, D. "Demons, Demonology." In *Encyclopedia Judaica*, vol. 5. Jerusalem: Macmillan, 1971, pp. 1521–1526.

Huels, J. "A Juridical Notion of Sacramentals." *StC* 38 (2004): pp. 345–368.

Kee, H. "The Terminology of Mark's Exorcism Stories." *New Testament Studies* 14 (1967): pp. 232–246.

Lowe, E. A. "The Vatican MS of the Gelasian Sacramentary and Its Supplement at Paris." *Journal for Theological Studies* 27, no. 108 (July 1926), p. 357–373.

National Conference of Catholic Bishops. "New Rite of Exorcism." *Committee on the Liturgy Newsletter* 35 (1999): pp. 58–60.

Petersen, A. K. "The Notion of Demon: Open Questions to a Diffuse Concept." In *Die Dämonen*, ed. A. Lange, H. Lichtenberger, and K. F. Diethard Römheld. Tübingen: Mohr Siebeck, 2002.

Reese, D. "Demons: New Testament." In *The Anchor Bible Dictionary*, vol. 2, pp. 140–142. New York, NY: Doubleday, 1992.

Van Slyke, D. G. "The Ancestry and Theology of the Rite of Major Exorcism (1999/2004)." *Antiphon* 10, no. 1 (2006): pp. 70–116.

——. "The Human Agents of Exorcism in the Early Christian Period: All Christians, Any Christians, or a Select Few Christians?" *Antiphon* 16, no. 3 (2012): pp. 179–223.

Freemasonry References

Anderson, J. *The Constitutions of the Free-Masons*. 1734. Repr., London: Forgotten Books, 2019.

Benedict XIV. Bull *Providas Romanorum*. March 18, 1751.

Clement XII. Bull on the Condemnation of Freemasonry *In eminenti*. April 28, 1738.

Code of Canon Law: Latin-English Edition. 1st ed. CLSA, 1983.

Congregation for the Doctrine of the Faith. Declaration Concerning Status of Catholics Becoming Freemasons. February 17, 1981.

——. Declaration on Masonic Associations. November 26, 1983.

Gregory XVI. Encyclical on Liberalism and Religious Indifferentism *Mirari vos*. August 15, 1832.

Leo XII. Encyclical on Secret Societies *Quo graviora*. March 13, 1826.

Leo XIII. Encyclical on Freemasonry *Humanum genus*. April 20, 1884.

Master Mason Edition of the Holy Bible. Wichita, KS: Heirloom Bible, 1991.

Peters, E., ed. *The 1917 Pio-Benedictine Code of Canon Law*. San Francisco: Ignatius Press, 2001.

Pike, A. *Morals and Dogma of the Ancient and Accepted Scottish Rite of Freemasonry*. 1872. Washington DC: Supreme Council of the Thirty-Third Degree, 1964.

Pius VII. Bull *Ecclesiam a Jesu Christo*. September 13, 1821.

——. Encyclical on His Program for His Pontificate *Traditi humilitati*. May 24, 1829.

Pius IX. Encyclical on Faith and Religion *Qui pluribus*. November 9, 1846.

Salza, J. *Masonry Unmasked: An Insider Reveals the Secrets of the Lodge*. Huntington, IN: Our Sunday Visitor, 2006.

——. *Why Catholics Cannot Be Masons*. Rockford, IL: TAN, 2008.

Whalen, W. J. *Christianity and American Freemasonry*, William J. Whalen. Milwaukee, WI: Bruce, 1958.

Appendix

Medical and Mental Illness

+

After reading and reflecting on the history of exorcism, it may be that some readers wonder whether their problems have a spiritual origin. If so, it is important to remember that ruling out the much more common mundane hypotheses (medical or mental illness, and misunderstandings) is critical.

The great majority of cases are based on misunderstandings, medical illness, or mental illness. Some cases involve a combination of a genuine spiritual problem and medical or mental illness, and most genuine demonic cases have at least some disturbance in the emotions or thinking. Some cases are clearly a spiritual problem, and there is less mundane distress in the person or their lives, as seen mostly in cases of possession of a devout Catholic with a supportive family.

By jumping to the hypothesis that the problem is spiritual, a person can leave untreated some progressive medical problem that needs to be addressed (like a brain tumor or the onset of mental illness).

While it is true that most requests for assistance are based on mundane problems, there are genuine spiritually based cases. Schizophrenia doesn't make you suddenly fluent in ancient languages. Epilepsy doesn't make you suddenly know the details of the secret sins of the people in the room. A sleep disorder doesn't make you able to always identify the one blessed object in a set of objects.

Some of the commonly misunderstood medical and mental illnesses follow.

Sleep disorders account for most complaints of negative spiritual activity. Always be alert to problems that occur exclusively when tired, going to sleep, or waking from sleep. When moving into or out of sleep, people pass through a state of consciousness where they can dream while they are partly awake. They are not aware that they are dreaming, and so these experiences seem real. These are called hypnopompic hallucinations when coming out of sleep, and hypnagogic hallucinations when going into sleep. Some people also have sleep paralysis, a malfunction of the natural immobilization of the body during sleep. This leads to the condition where the person is partly awake, paralyzed from the nose down, and seeing things. It is a very fearful experience in which the person can look around but cannot scream or move their body.

It is common for people with schizophrenia to interpret the voices they hear as demons. This is particularly true when they first have their psychotic break. It is important to work in concert with their family and treatment team to encourage them to cooperate with treatment (medication). Praying over someone with schizophrenia can reinforce the delusion that they are possessed and so can cause harm. For this reason, it is helpful to have some experience with mental illness when doing the intake interviews.

Cervical dystonia can cause body contortions and grimaces of the facial muscles.

Tourettes disorder can cause loud verbal outbursts of profanity and intrusive thoughts of violent and disturbing images.

Epilepsy of various types, which can cause strange experiences and convulsions.

Hysteria is fear, and eventually panic, accentuated by other people. With the popularity of paranormal television shows and movies, it is not uncommon to find people that are hypersensitized to sounds or temperature changes due to a fear of ghosts or demons. In some cases, parents encourage this fear in their young children, who then subconsciously go along with the idea to please their parents.

It is common that women in older age experience strange bodily sensations caused by hormone changes. These are often in the reproductive organs. When this is combined with early onset senility, dementia, or general mental decline, the person may become fixated on a demonic hypothesis to explain her experiences.

There are many mental issues that can arise from the use of, or withdrawal from, legal and illegal drugs. It is also not uncommon for older people to make errors in taking their medications and have psychosis as a side-effect of this. There have been a number of cases where modern synthetic drugs (K2, spice, etc.) have caused dramatic psychotic experiences that were interpreted as possession.

There are many things that can affect the brain, causing psychotic experiences (a break with reality). A spiritual complaint could be based on the onset of schizophrenia, depression with psychotic symptoms, manic depression with psychotic symptoms, a brain tumor, drug effects, or an infection. There are a number of other brain-based problems that can cause false experiences and paranoid fears.

Some people that have had a head or spine injury attribute their pains, tingling, and other sensations to spiritual attacks.

There can be a psychotic tinge to these cases where the person is very resistant to any other hypothesis about their symptoms, no matter how reasonable.

Malingering is when a person pretends to be sick in order to get attention. Some people see the special attention people get on television shows and so use complaints about spirits to become the center of attention. This sometimes happens with young children also.

Factitious disorder is when a person pretends to be sick for practical gain. These situations are rare. In one case, the cover story of ghost molestations was used by a sex offender to cover up their crimes in the home. In another case, a person wanted to use demonic infestation as a defense to avoid conviction for a gun crime.

At the edge of the retina, there is only black and white vision and little detail. Since the nervous system does not work perfectly at all times, this leads to the occasional perception of a black and white vague shadow at the edge of vision. When the person turns to look at it, bringing the full detailed color vision of the middle of the retina to bear, it "disappears."

It is not uncommon for mentally healthy people to hear voices or other meaningful sounds in white noise: the running of a vacuum, for instance. People with some psychotic problems are more prone to this.

It is fairly common for people developing dementia to have delusions, hallucinations, and behavioral disturbances. If they have a strong religious worldview, this can be interpreted by them as a spiritual attack or possession.

People sometimes blame regular life problems or mental illness on curses or demonic activity. This externalizes problems for them. They often read extensively on possession and exorcism, both online and in books, and self-diagnose their problems. These cases can take on a sad desperation where a person goes from diocese to diocese demanding that they have an exorcism based on their self-diagnosis, while rejecting any other hypothesis.

Some complaints are genuine spiritual problems, coexisting along with medical or mental issues. These problems can be unrelated or secondary to the spiritual problem. It is typical for people living in demonically infested homes to get very little sleep and spend their time at home in great anxiety. This often leads to irritability and mild depression. It is also common that with oppression and possession, people develop some depression, anxiety, and sometimes medical problems secondary to the spiritual affliction.

Every case is unique and there is no simple way to discern all of these possibilities. The medical and mental checkup is an essential step. Leaving a medical or mental illness untreated because a person feels their issues are demonic is irresponsible and can lead to harm. Having a person under some medical supervision while spiritual issues are addressed is the best course of action in cases of possession. In many house cases, there is no obvious medical or mental problem, and the complaints are resolved in one or two visits, so medical supervision is usually not needed.

About the Author

✠

Adam Blai is a Church-decreed expert on religious demonology and exorcism for the Diocese of Pittsburgh. He has helped train exorcists for over more than fifteen years and has attended hundreds of solemn exorcisms. His journey started in brain-wave research and psychology and is now focused on the spiritual realities of miracles, angels, demons, and possession. He is the author of several books, including *The Exorcism Files.*

Sophia Institute

Sophia Institute is a nonprofit institution that seeks to nurture the spiritual, moral, and cultural life of souls and to spread the gospel of Christ in conformity with the authentic teachings of the Roman Catholic Church.

Sophia Institute Press fulfills this mission by offering translations, reprints, and new publications that afford readers a rich source of the enduring wisdom of mankind.

Sophia Institute also operates the popular online resource CatholicExchange.com. *Catholic Exchange* provides world news from a Catholic perspective as well as daily devotionals and articles that will help readers to grow in holiness and live a life consistent with the teachings of the Church.

In 2013, Sophia Institute launched Sophia Institute for Teachers to renew and rebuild Catholic culture through service to Catholic education. With the goal of nurturing the spiritual, moral, and cultural life of souls, and an abiding respect for the role and work of teachers, we strive to provide materials and programs that are at once enlightening to the mind and ennobling to the heart; faithful and complete, as well as useful and practical.

Sophia Institute gratefully recognizes the Solidarity Association for preserving and encouraging the growth of our apostolate over the course of many years. Without their generous and timely support, this book would not be in your hands.

www.SophiaInstitute.com
www.CatholicExchange.com
www.SophiaInstituteforTeachers.org

Sophia Institute Press is a registered trademark of Sophia Institute.
Sophia Institute is a tax-exempt institution as defined by the Internal Revenue Code, Section 501(c)(3). Tax ID 22-2548708.